ASYLUM SEEKERS

Huntersville, Carolina del Norte, EEUU, November 3 2018

First published by Juan Rodulfo
Copyright © 2018 by Juan Rodulfo
All rights reserved.
No part of this publication may be reproduced, stored or transmitted in any form or by any means, electronic, mechanical, photocopying, recording, scanning or otherwise without written permission from the publisher. It is illegal to copy this book, publish it on a website, or distribute it by any other means without permission.
Juan Rodulfo has no responsibility for the persistence or accuracy of URLs of external or third-party Internet websites referenced in this publication and does not warrant that the content of such websites is, or will remain, accurate or appropriate. The names used by companies to distinguish their products are often claimed as trademarks. All trademarks and product names used in this book and on its cover, trade names, service marks, trademarks are trademarks of their respective owners. The publishers and the book are not associated with any products or suppliers mentioned in this book. None of the companies or organizations referenced in the book have endorsed it.
Library of Congress Catalog
Names: Rodulfo, Juan
ISBN: 9781730884634 (paperback)
ISBN: 9798330453207 (e-book)
ISBN: 9798330453191 (hardcover)
First edition
Layout by Juan Rodulfo
Cover art by Juan Rodulfo
Production: Aussie Trading, LLC
books@aussietrading.ltd
Printed in the USA

theasylumseekers.com

"Humans are the only species on earth that hunts, tortures and murders to their equals for pleasure."

theasylumseekers.com

Content

PREFACE	11
DEFINITION	17
The right to asylum	18
Medieval England	19
Modern political asylum	23
RELEVANT FACTS	26
AMERICA	37
United States	37
The "Caravans"	38
Detention Centers	45
Immigration Courts in the United States	51
EUROPE AND AFRICA	54
European Union	54
France	54
United Kingdom	57
Deaths in the Mediterranean	58
OCEANIA AND ASIA	63
Myanmar Rohingya: What you need to know about the crisis	63
Who are the Rohingya?	63
Why are they fleeing?	64
What is the magnitude of the crisis?	65
VENEZUELA	67
Report on Human Rights in Venezuela 2017	67
Amnesty International Report 2017/18: Venezuela	70
Background	71
Freedom of expression	72
Freedom of Assembly	72
Excessive use of force	73
Arbitrary arrests and detentions	75
Torture and ill-treatment	76
Human rights defenders	77
Justice System	78

- Prisoners of Conscience 79
- International Scrutiny 79
- Enforced Disappearances 80
- Impunity 81
- Detention 81
- Right to Food 82
- Right to Health 83
- Women's Rights 83
- Sexual and Reproductive Rights 84
- Refugees and Asylum Seekers 84
- Human Rights Watch País Sumario: Venezuela 85
- US sanctions 96
  - Executive Orders: 97
- BUREAUCRACY 99
  - The Universal Declaration of Human Rights 99
    - Preamble 99
    - United States 109
    - Immigration and Nationality Act of 1965 110
    - Europe 123
    - South Africa 126
    - Australia 132
- THE AUTHOR 137
  - Publications: 138
    - Books: 138
    - Blogs: 139
  - Audiovisual Productions: 139
    - Podcasts: 139
    - Music: 139
    - Photography & Video: 139
  - Social Media Profiles: 139
  - Where to get Juan Rodulfo's books: 140
  - Other publications by the Author ...... **Error! Bookmark not defined.**
    - Remain SILENT, the only right we have. The Legal Aliens ....**Error! Bookmark not defined.**
    - Gorilla Handbook: 9 Rules for Being the "Fer-Pecto" Dictator ....**Error! Bookmark not defined.**

theasylumseekers.com

Why Maslow?..............**Error! Bookmark not defined.**
Endnotes..142

NOTE TO THE FIRST EDITION: The second part of this book was entitled: **REMAIN SILENT,** The only right we have. The legal Aliens, published in 2023 the English version and 2024 the Spanish version.

PREFACE

What is wrong with humans? Is there anyone out there in Governments or Circles of Power with any sense of respect for Planet Earth and its Inhabitants?

It is currently 2018, I have been living in the United States since I was forced, along with Yohana, my wife, and Sofia, our 7-year-old daughter, to flee the country I was born and raised in 2014, leaving behind Parents, Siblings, Family, friends, dreams, and much of our hearts.

It was in July 2014, when my wife and I began selling our belongings to raise funds for the trip, quietly to avoid alerting our pursuers and to keep our parents and friends free from further worry. Due to the growing socio-economic disaster caused by the pseudo "Bolivarian Revolution", we couldn't find a flight together, so my wife and daughter left the country via Colombia-New York at the end of September, staying behind for a couple of weeks and then flying via Mexico-Miami.

This couple of weeks was one of the longest I have ever experienced, without access to cell phones to communicate with them, barely WhatsApp when they find access to WiFi, with concerns about how Yohana and Sofia would be, first if they could leave our country Venezuela, then transit through Colombia and finally if they could reach U.S. territory or would be deported or detained. Alone at home trying to focus, be optimistic and distract myself a little, I decided to rent Matt Damon and Jodie Foster's film Elysium: "In 2154, the Earth is overpopulated and polluted. Most of Earth's citizens live in poverty, on the brink of starvation, and with little technology and health care. The rich and powerful live in Elysium, a gigantic space habitat in Earth's orbit. Elysium is technologically advanced, with devices like Med-Bays that can cure all diseases, reverse the aging process, and regenerate parts of the body. There is a long-running dispute between Elysium and Earth, whose residents want Elysium's technology to cure their diseases. Max Da Costa (Matt Damon), a former car thief on probation, lives in the ruins of Los Angeles and works on an assembly line for Armadyne Corp. Led by CEO John Carlyle, who originally designed Elysium, Armadyne Corp. produces Elysium's weaponry, as well as the robots that guard the land. During an industrial accident at the factory, Max is trapped in a microwave oven and is exposed to a lethal dose of radiation. After being rescued, he is informed that he has five days to live before succumbing to radiation poisoning. Desperate for a cure, he and his friend Julio seek the help of a human smuggler named Spider to bring him to Elysium; Their only chance of survival is to use a Med-Bay.

Meanwhile, when three ships carrying illegal immigrants from Earth attempt to reach Elysium, Secretary of Defense Delacourt (Jodie Foster) orders sleeper agent Kruger to destroy the shuttles. As two of the shuttles are shot down into space, killing everyone on board, the third shuttle evades the missiles. However, once on Elysium, everyone on board is killed or deported.

Spider agrees to take Max to Elysium if he can steal financial information from Carlyle. To help him, Spider's men surgically fitted Max with an electrical exoskeleton. In the end, Spider and Max reach the core of Elysium's computer, where Spider realizes that activating the program will kill Max. Max personally activates the program, having last spoken to Frey over the radio. When Max dies, Elysium's computer core reboots and registers all of Earth's residents as Elysian citizens. President Patel arrives with security guards, but the robots refuse to arrest Spider, whom they now recognize as a citizen. "Matilda is cured with a Med-Bay computer and Elysium sends a huge fleet of medical ships to begin treating the people of Earth."

Of course, I was not Matt Damon or Yohana Jodie Foster, but the story was the same as we were living at that time, large numbers of the population dying for lack of food, medicine and disease, suffering violence and being persecuted by governments or criminal organizations, fleeing away from their original spaces to the South of the South Earth to these "developed countries"[i] of the Northern Hemisphere in search of saving their lives to find the Incarceration, Racism and Harassment of some government officials. Thankfully, I was home alone to hide my tears of frustration from my wife and daughter.

Helped by two of my best friends, both former officers of the Venezuelan Army who found themselves seeking asylum in the U.S., after being accused as "Enemies of the Revolution", by the Dictatorship that rules that piece of land called Venezuela, my family and I found shelter, food, work and thanks to having learned English we filled out our own asylum application.

It was 2015, after my arrival, I met up again with a former student and friend, who needed help finding shelter, food, clothing, furniture, work, a car, and guidance to submit her asylum application in English. My wife and I already have all these connections saved and ready to share: Refuge: the Community in which we already lived as interpreters; Food & Clothing: Ada Jenkins and Lydia's Loft Nonprofits in this zip code; Medical Care: Lake Norman Free Clinic; Guidance for Applying for a Driver's License and Car: A

Couple of "Buy Here-Pay Here" Friends Used Car Businesses in Charlotte, NC. Then a family member arrived, another relative, a friend of a friend, it was 2017; the population of asylum seekers was growing at a rapid pace and I published the website asiloenusa.info, to have and share in one place information on how to apply for asylum, News from around the world, and News from the United States Immigration Office (USCIS).

At the time of publishing this book (November 2018), we have met and assisted more than one hundred Venezuelan families in their asylum applications, including one from Ecuador and one from Colombia. This same year, two "Caravans", around 7 thousand people of low economic resources forced by the Violence of Criminal Organizations, Abusive Governments and Poverty walk from their original spaces in Central America and Mexico in search of saving their lives in the United States.

On the other side of Planet Earth, more than 100,000 people in the same or worse conditions of the "Caravans", risk their lives by crossing the Mediterranean Sea from Africa to Europe, causing the death of large percentages of this population, by starvation or drowning.

WHAT'S WRONG WITH HUMANS?

OH! turn the Earth Globe a little to the left and we will get the Genocide of the Rohingya by the Myanmar Army.

The list goes on so I got tired of the concepts of "Government", "Nationalism", "Patriotism", "Flags", "Citizenship", "Currencies", all this related to the oppression of the majority by a few who hide behind Corporate Names called Countries with all their individual concepts of "Homeland", prompting me to publish this research on Asylum and Why Maslow? (visit: porquemaslow.com), where I try to address poverty as a result of government-corporate policies based on Maslow's Theory.

1

DEFINITION

The Collins Dictionary defines political asylum as: "The right to live in a foreign country and the government of that country grants it to people who have to leave their own country for political reasons." It also says, "Political asylum is "The right to live in a foreign country, and is granted by the government of that country to people who have to leave their own country because they are in danger of persecution."

English: political asylum

Portuguese-Brazilian: political asylum

Chino: 政治避难

European Spanish: political asylum

Frances: political asylum

Alemán: political asylum

Italian: political asylum

Japan: 政治亡命者の保護

Koreano: 정치적 망명

theasylumseekers.com

European Portuguese: political asylum

English: political asylum[ii]

The right to asylum

The right of asylum (sometimes called the right of political asylum, from the ancient Greek word ἄσυλον) is an ancient legal concept, according to which a person persecuted by one's own country can be protected by another sovereign authority, such as another country or ecclesiastical official, who in medieval times could offer sanctuary. This right was already recognized by the Egyptians, the Greeks and the Hebrews, from whom it was adopted in the Western tradition. René Descartes fled to the Netherlands, Voltaire to England, and Thomas Hobbes to France, because each state offered protection to persecuted foreigners.

The Egyptians, Greeks, and Hebrews recognized a religious "right of asylum," protecting criminals (or those accused of crimes) from legal action to some extent. This principle was later adopted by the established Christian church, and several rules were developed detailing how to qualify for protection and what degree of protection you would receive.

The Council of Orléans decided in 511, in the presence of Clovis I, that asylum could be granted to anyone who took refuge in a church or church property, or in the house of a bishop. This protection was extended to murderers, thieves, and adulterers alike.

That "Everyone has the right to seek and enjoy in other countries asylum from persecution" is enshrined in the 1948 United Nations Universal Declaration of Human Rights and is supported by the 1951 Convention relating to the Status of Refugees and the 1967 Protocol relating to the Status of Refugees. Under these agreements, a refugee is a person who is outside the territory of that person's country for fear of persecution on protected grounds, such as race, caste, nationality, religion, political opinions, and participation in any particular social group or social activity.

Medieval England

In England, King Æthelberht of Kent proclaimed the first Anglo-Saxon laws on sanctuary in about 600 AD. However, Geoffrey of Monmouth in his Historia Regum Britanniae (c. 1136) says that the legendary pre-Saxon king Dunvallo Molmutius (4th/5th century BC) enacted sanctuary laws among the Laws of Molmutine as recorded by Gildas (c. 500–570). The term "grith"[iiii] was used by the laws of King Ethelred. In the Norman era that followed 1066, two types of sanctuary had evolved: all churches had the lower-level powers and could grant a sanctuary within the church proper, but the broader powers of churches licensed by royal statute extended the sanctuary to an area around the church. At least twenty-two churches had charters for this wider sanctuary, including:

- Battle Abbey
- Beverley
- Colchester
- Durham, England
- Hexham
- Norwich
- Ripon
- Wells Cathedral
- Winchester Cathedral
- Westminster Monastery
- York Minster

Sometimes, the offender had to come to the chapel to protect himself, or ring a bell, hold a ring or someone knocking on the door, or sit on a certain chair ("banqueta"). Some of these items survive in several churches. In other places, the sanctuary is located in an area around the church or abbey, sometimes extending over a radius of up to a mile and a half. Stone "sanctuary crosses" marked the boundaries of the area; Some crosses still exist as well. It could therefore become a race between the criminal and medieval law enforcement officers to the edge of the nearest shrine. Serving justice in the foot fleet could be a difficult proposition.

The sanctuaries of the church were regulated by common law. An asylum seeker had to confess his sins, surrender his weapons, and allow supervision by a church or abbey organization with jurisdiction. The seekers had forty days to decide whether to surrender to the secular authorities and be tried for their alleged crimes, or confess their guilt, leave the kingdom, go into exile by the shortest route, and never return without the king's permission. Those who returned faced execution under the law and/or excommunication from the Church.

If the suspects decided to confess their guilt and abjure themselves, they did so in a public ceremony, usually at the doors of the church. They would turn their possessions over to the church, and any land ownership to the crown. The coroner, a medieval official, would then choose a port city from which the fugitive should leave England (although the fugitive sometimes had this privilege). The fugitive came out barefoot and with his head uncovered, carrying a wooden cane as a symbol of protection under the church. Theoretically, they would stay on the main road, arrive at the port and take the first ship out of England. In practice, however, the fugitive could move away to a safe distance, leave the space limited by the cross, and begin a new life. However, one can safely assume that the victim's friends and family knew about this ploy and would do everything they could to make sure this didn't happen; or even that the fugitives never made it to their intended port of call, becoming victims of vigilante justice under the guise of a fugitive wandering too far from the main road while trying to "escape."

Knowing the bleak options, some fugitives rejected both options and chose to escape asylum before the forty days were up. Others simply made no choice and did nothing. Since it was illegal for the victim's friends to enter an asylum, the church would deprive the fugitive of food and water until a decision was made.

Henry VIII changed the asylum rules, reducing to a short list the types of crimes for which people could apply for asylum. The medieval asylum system was finally abolished altogether by James I in 1623.

During the Wars of the Roses, when the Yorkists or Lancastrians gained the advantage of winning a battle, some followers on the losing side might find themselves surrounded by followers on the other side and would not be able to return to their own side. Realizing this situation, they would rush to take shelter in the nearest church until it was safe to leave. A good example is Queen Elizabeth Woodville, consort of Edward IV of England.

In 1470, when the Lancasters briefly restored Henry VI to the throne, Queen Elizabeth was living in London with several daughters. She moved with them to Westminster for refuge, living there in royal comfort until Edward IV was restored to the throne in 1471 and gave birth to her first son Edward V during that time. When King Edward IV died in 1483, Elizabeth (who was very unpopular even with Yorkists and probably needed protection) took her five daughters and youngest son (Richard, Duke of York) and moved back to Westminster Sanctuary. To make sure it had all the comforts of home, she brought in so much furniture and so many chests that the workers had to poke holes in some of the walls to get everything fast enough to fit her.

Modern political asylum

Article 14 of the Universal Declaration of Human Rights states that "Everyone has the right to seek and enjoy asylum from persecution in other countries." The 1951 United Nations Convention relating to the Status of Refugees and the 1967 Protocol relating to the Status of Refugees guide national legislation relating to political asylum. Under these agreements, a refugee (or for cases where the basic means of repression has been applied directly or environmentally to the refugee) is a person who is outside the territory of that person's own country (or place of habitual residence if stateless) due to fear of persecution on protected land. Protected grounds include race, caste, nationality, religion, political opinions, and membership and/or participation in any particular social group or social activities. The surrender of true victims of persecution to their persecutor is a violation of a principle called non-refoulement[iv], part of the customary and trucial Law of Nations.[v].

These are the terms and criteria accepted as principles and a fundamental part in the non-refoulement order of the 1951 United Nations Convention relating to the Status of Refugees.

Since the 1990s, victims of sexual persecution (which can include domestic violence, or the systematic oppression of a gender or sexual minority) have been accepted in some countries as a legitimate category for asylum claims, when claimants can prove that the state is unable or unwilling to provide protection.

2

RELEVANT FACTS

On June 18, 2018, Sadof Alexander posted online: 8 Dangerous Myths About Refugees Debunked[vi]:

Myth 1: Most of the world's refugees are in rich countries
There is a belief that the United States and many European countries host a large number of refugees. In reality, the majority of the world's refugees live in poor or middle-income countries. The UN Refugee Agency estimates that more than eight out of ten of the world's refugees are protected by developing countries. Turkey, Pakistan and Lebanon hosted the largest number of refugees in mid-2016. These three countries combined have 5.4 million refugees.

Myth 2: Most refugees are adults.
Becoming a refugee is an incredibly difficult situation for anyone, but even more so for children. More than half of all refugees are children. That's almost one in every 200 children in the world. Many of these children are separated

from their parents, which means that these children must take care of themselves and even handle their own legal cases.

Myth 3: Refugees and migrants are the same.
Although the two terms are sometimes used interchangeably, refugees and migrants are separate and distinct terms. Refugees are people who cannot return to their homes safely and seek protection from dangerous situations. The term "refugee" comes with a specific legal context that does not apply to all migrants.

As the UN Refugee Agency puts it, "the combination of 'refugees' and 'migrant' can undermine public support for refugees and the asylum institution at a time when more refugees need such protection than ever before."

Myth 4: All refugees come from war zones.
While most of the refugees in history have come out of war, other issues also contribute to the refugee crisis.
Persecution is one of the most common reasons, which can take many forms. Religious, social, national, racial, and political persecution has led to refugees.
Rising hunger is another factor that has contributed to the crisis. Severe droughts in North Africa have created food

instability, leading to millions of people being displaced in search of a reliable source of food.

Myth 5: It's easy for refugees to resettle in other countries

The difference between shelter and resettlement has a huge impact on refugees. Resettlement ensures that refugees have legal and physical protection, including access to rights and services similar to those of nationals. By the end of 2016, less than 1% of refugees were resettled in other countries. That means that less than 1% of refugees are legally entitled to receive valuable resources from the nation in which they are located.

Myth 6: Refugees are an economic burden on other countries.

Despite concerns that refugees will pose financial problems to the nations they resettle to, research has found that accepting refugees actually boosts national economies. Some experts have argued that although the upfront cost of resettlement can be high, accepting refugees is a good investment in a nation's financial future.

Professor Alexander Betts of the University of Oxford points to Uganda, for example. "In Kampala, the capital city, for example, we found that 21 percent of refugees have businesses that employ other people and 40 percent of those employees are citizens of the host country. In other words, refugees were creating jobs. "Many of the companies were, even in the refugee camps, highly innovative and networked in the structures of the global economy."

Moreover, in the United States, the average refugee becomes a net contributor to the public coffers eight years after arrival. One study found that refugees actually pay more in taxes than they receive in benefits, about $21,000 more in the first 20 years in the United States.

Myth 7: Once a refugee is resettled in another country, things become easier

The battle refugees face doesn't end once they settle in a new country. After resettlement, refugees encounter many problems in their new countries. These can include trauma, language barriers, financial issues, discrimination, and access to education. These obstacles can be even more difficult for children, who face great challenges at a very young age.

Myth 8: There's nothing you can do to help the refugee crisis

In such a massive global situation, it may feel like one person can't make a difference, but this is not true. Every day people can do a lot to help refugees. Volunteering, awareness, petitions, donations, and more can be done to help those affected by the refugee crisis.

More numbers and facts were published in this article by the Refugee Council[vii]:

Here are our top 20 facts based on the latest asylum statistics.

1. The world is in the grip of one of the largest refugee crises in history. Around 60 million people around the world have been forced to flee their homes.
2. It is the poor countries, not the rich ones, the Western countries, that take care of the vast majority of the world's refugees. The UN Refugee Agency estimates that 86% of the world's refugees are protected by developing countries.
Lebanon, a country half the size of Wales, single-handedly hosts the same number of refugees who fled across Europe last year.
3. The terrible scenes we are seeing in the Mediterranean and across Europe are a symptom of this wider crisis. But make no mistake, this is a refugee crisis. According to the UN Refugee Agency, 84% of those who arrived in Europe during 2015 came from the world's top 10 refugee-producing countries.

4. With the world in the grip of the biggest refugee crisis since World War II, comparatively few people can reach Britain in their search for safety.

    Last year, more than 1.2 million people sought safety in Europe; almost double the number of applicants for protection in 2014. However, Britain received only 38,878 asylum applications, including dependents.

5. Britain is not the main recipient of asylum applications in Europe. Germany, Sweden, France, Hungary, Italy and Austria receive significantly more applications than Britain's Refugee Council. Britain also receives fewer applications than Belgium, the Netherlands and Switzerland and slightly more than Finland.

    Together, Germany and Hungary receive more than half of all applications submitted in the EU.

    Britain received just 3% of all asylum applications filed in the EU last year.

    Britain's Refugee Council is ranked 17th in Europe in terms of asylum applications per capita.

6. That means more people arrived in Hungary in a single month last year than asylum in Britain during all of 2015.

7. Britain does not offer an asylum visa. In fact, there are very few legal ways for refugees to escape their country and apply for asylum in another country. The truth is that, when war breaks out, countries like Britain often close legal escape routes for refugees. Before the Syrian conflict broke out, less than 30% of Syrians' travel visa applications were rejected. In 2015, this shot up to almost 50%.
Refugees don't put their lives in the hands of smugglers because they want to. They do it because they often have no choice.

8. This lack of safe and legal routes for refugees to reach safety and apply for asylum has deadly results. In 2015, 3,771 men, women and children lost their lives during their desperate attempt to cross the Mediterranean Sea. Each death was a tragedy. So far this year, more than 400 people have died.

9. World events often relate directly to asylum claims. Ongoing unrest in the Middle East and South Sudan and a sustained wave of people fleeing tyranny in Eritrea led to increases in applications from those nationalities. The top 5 nationalities that applied for asylum in Britain last year were:
    - Eritrean
    - Iranian

- Sudanese
- Syrian
- Pakistani

10. Asylum seekers make up a small proportion of new arrivals in Britain. Today's statistics show that 617,000 people arrived in Britain in the year to September 2015; asylum seekers who came to Britain to escape persecution accounted for just 6% of that figure. Of course, not all asylum seekers will be allowed to stay in Britain.

11. 39% of the initial decisions made last year were grants of some form of protection.

12. However, many refugees had to rely on the courts rather than the government to provide them with the protection they needed. The proportion of asylum applications allowed in 2015 rose to 35% from 28% in 2014.

13. In 2015, Britain's Refugee Council witnessed a stunning increase in the rejection rate of Eritrean asylum seekers due to the unreliable new guidelines used by the Home Office.

These guidelines have been widely discredited, but the Home Office refuses to revise them. Meanwhile, many Eritrean refugees are forced to rely on the courts to provide them with the protection they need. In late 2015, courts overturned a staggering 90 per cent of denials of Eritrea's claims that were appealed.

14. Unaccompanied children were much less likely than adults to receive refugee protection. Overall, 34% of decisions on asylum applications were specifically asylum grants, compared to only 27% of separated children. Instead, many separated children are granted short-term leave to stay, which expires after 2.5 years.

15. The number of Syrian refugees resettled in Britain was just 1,337 since the conflict began. The government has promised to resettle 20,000 Syrian refugees by 2020. That's only 4,000 a year. There are 4.7 million Syrian refugees.

16. The number of Syrians who have sought asylum in Britain since the conflict began stands at just 7,594. In 2015 alone, more than 388,000 Syrians have arrived in Europe by sea. Like most of the world's refugees, very few Syrians arrive in Britain in search of safety.

17. The backlog of cases pending a decision increased to 26,409, 15% more than in 2014. Each of these cases represents a trapped person living in limbo, anxiously awaiting news of their fate.

18. At the end of 2015, the government was supporting 34,363 asylum-seekers and their dependents. This figure has increased every quarter since the end of September 2012, but is still below the figure at the end of 2003, when 80,123 asylum seekers were supported. This does not mean that asylum seekers live in luxury; far from there; People have no say in the place where they live and are often left to survive on around £5 a day.

19. In 2015, 14,751 asylum-seekers were locked up in detention centres at some point. Shamefully, more than a third of all asylum seekers are detained during the asylum process. Despite the government's 2010 pledge to end immigration detention of children, 128 children were incarcerated during this time. Two-thirds of the children who left detention were released, making their detention not only harmful but futile.

20. In the last year, only 670 non-Syrian refugees were resettled in Britain through programmes run in conjunction with the UN Refugee Agency (UNHCR). A truly unfortunate number given that other countries resettle thousands of refugees. *UNHCR estimates that there are around 1*

million refugees worldwide who are in desperate need of a resettlement place.

3

AMERICA

United States

The United States recognizes individuals' right to asylum as specified by international and federal law. A specific number of legally defined refugees applying for refugee status abroad, as well as those applying for asylum after arriving in the United States, are admitted annually.

As noted in the article specifically on asylum and refugees in the United States, since World War II, more refugees have found homes in the United States than any other nation and more than two million refugees have arrived in the United States since 1980. For much of the 1990s, the United States accepted more than 100,000 refugees per year, although this figure has recently declined to around 50,000 per year in the first decade of the 21st century, due to heightened security concerns. As for asylum seekers, the latest statistics show that 86,400 people sought refuge in the United States in 2001. Prior to the September 11 attacks, individual asylum seekers were screened in private proceedings at the U.S. Immigration and Naturalization Services (INS).

Despite this, concerns have been raised regarding the U.S. asylum and refugee determination processes. A recent empirical analysis by three legal scholars described the U.S. asylum process as a game of refugee roulette; that is, the outcome of asylum determinations depends largely on the personality of the particular adjudicator to whom an application is randomly assigned, rather than on the merits of the case. The very low number of Iraqi refugees accepted between 2003 and 2007 exemplifies concerns about U.S. refugee processes. The Foreign Policy Association reported that "Perhaps the most puzzling component of the refugee crisis in Iraq ... has been the inability of the U.S. To absorb more Iraqis after the invasion of the country in 2003. To date, the U.S. has granted fewer than 800 Iraqi refugee status, only 133 in 2007. By contrast, the United States granted asylum to more than 100,000 Vietnamese refugees during the Vietnam War."[viii]

The "Caravans"

David Nakamura and Nick Miroff, wrote the following article in the Washington Post on November 1, 2018: President Trump said on Thursday that he will try to take executive action next week to end the "abuse" of the U.S. asylum system, a plan that could include tents "at the southern border with the goal of holding migrants indefinitely and making it harder for them to stay at the U.S. country.

But Trump offered some other details during remarks at the White House, where he reiterated unsubstantiated claims he has made in recent weeks that a caravan of migrants from Central America, traveling north through Mexico on foot, poses an urgent threat to national security. He characterized the group, which includes many families with children, as dangerous and akin to an "invasion."

The president's remarks, broadcast live on cable, came days before Tuesday's mid-Tuesday election, Trump's latest bid to make immigration the main issue of the campaign.

Trump said the emergency measures he plans to take would protect the U.S. against what he called rampant fraud that threatens to overwhelm the nation's immigration system.

The president offered no legal justification for his plan, and dismissed questions about the legality of some of the methods he suggested could be employed, such as detaining families indefinitely or refusing migrants a hearing in immigration court.

Such moves will likely trigger legal challenges from civil rights groups.

Trump also suggested that U.S. military members at the border could shoot caravan members if migrants throw rocks at soldiers.

Lawyers for the White House, the Department of Homeland Security and the Department of Justice have fought in recent weeks to bring the president's sweeping demands to suspend humanitarian protections in line with U.S. laws that protect the right to seek refuge on U.S. soil, regardless of how the asylum seeker arrives on U.S. soil.

"These illegal caravans will not be allowed in the United States," Trump said. "They should come back now. They are wasting their time."

In a sign that the administration is moving to comply with Trump's orders, DHS has asked the Pentagon to provide up to 8,000 family detention beds at two sites, an administration official confirmed to The Washington Post on Thursday.

The president and his Republican allies have expressed confidence that Trump's hardline immigration message will motivate his conservative base as Republicans try to maintain control of Congress. Democrats have accused the president of stoking public fears about a pool of migrant families that has shrunk and remains 800 miles from the United States.

"The president's speech was a political stunt aimed at increasing fear and xenophobia days before the election," Rep. Bennie G. Thompson (Mississippi), the ranking Democrat on the House Homeland Security Committee, said in a statement.

Omar Jadwat, director of the American Civil Liberties Union's Immigrants' Rights Project, said Trump's lack of political details showed he was "trying to inflame his base in the run-up to the election."

In his remarks, Trump praised the troops, which the Pentagon said would act in supporting roles to help U.S. Border Patrol agents, who have the legal authority to make arrests.

Trump claimed that Mexican soldiers were "seriously injured" during clashes with a second group of migrants on the border with Guatemala last Sunday. "These are tough people. In many cases, there are young men, strong men," Trump said.

But the Mexican forces were federal police, not military, and there were no reports of serious injuries. When asked if the U.S. military would use lethal force, Trump suggested that troops would be forced to respond to violent confrontations.

"They want to throw stones at our military, our military is fighting back," Trump said. "We're going to consider, and I told them to consider it a rifle."

A Pentagon spokesman declined to specify how the military would react in the scenario set by Trump.

"We will not discuss hypothetical situations or specific measures within our rules on the use of force, but our forces are trained professionals who always have the inherent right to self-defense," said Lt. Col. Jamie Davis, a Pentagon spokesman. "I would also emphasize that our forces support DHS/CBP, which is conducting law enforcement activities."

News of Trump's comments reached the caravan Thursday night in Matias Romero Avendaño, Mexico, where migrants were camped out in a soggy sports field on the outskirts of the city.

"They won't shoot because we're not criminals," said Erik Miranda, 39. He said he had lived in the United States for 15 years and had been deported twice despite seeking asylum. "How horrible," Daniela Carbajal, 27, said when told of Trump's threat. "I'm not justifying stone-throwing, but remember: we have children among us."

Under the Refugee Act of 1980, migrants who present themselves at U.S. ports of entry or arrive on U.S. soil and state that they fear persecution in their home countries are entitled to a "credible fear" assessment. That review is usually done by a U.S. asylum officer. To determine if the applicant should be referred to an immigration judge.

If approved by the asylum officer, applicants are typically released into the United States while they await a hearing, which could take a year or more because immigration courts have a backlog of more than 750,000 cases.

Trump said large numbers of migrants are being trained by immigration lawyers to make bogus asylum claims and that more Central American families are making the journey because U.S. law prevents the federal government from detaining children for extended periods. The number of Central American families seeking asylum reached record levels this year.

The process, Trump claimed, "makes a mockery of our immigration system."

Legal analysts questioned the legality of draft plans, circulated within the Trump administration, that would issue blanket denials of asylum to large groups of immigrants, particularly those who do not arrive in the country through official ports of entry.

"You can't, by executive mandate, repeal an act of Congress or a constitutional amendment," said Deborah Anker, a professor at Harvard Law School. "He has to ask for new legislation."

Trump said the migrants in the caravan are not "legitimate" asylum seekers, arguing that the law should not be used to accommodate people fleeing poverty and is intended for those fleeing political and religious persecution.

The administration has already been trying to reduce asylum claims.

In recent months, U.S. Customs and Border Protection officers have turned away thousands of asylum seekers before they can file a claim, telling them to return later, usually citing capacity limits. The practice, known as "metering," is being challenged in federal court.

The caravan, a fluid and loosely organized group, numbered more than 7,000 at the beginning of last week, according to the United Nations, but the Mexican government's most recent estimates put the figure at about half. Other smaller collections of migrants have also been traveling north and attempting to join the main group.

Mexican authorities say more than 2,000 migrants have accepted his offer to seek asylum there and remain in southern Mexico.

If thousands of people in the caravan manage to reach the U.S. border. And they encounter severe restrictions on their ability to apply for asylum at legal crossings, it could significantly increase the chance that they will try to swim or float across the Rio Grande, even with thousands of

Border Patrol agents and U.S. soldiers waiting for them on the other side, experts warned.

It's unclear how they would be handled, but Trump has vowed not to release them into the U.S. while he awaits a court hearing, even though U.S. courts have limited the government's ability to hold children in immigration jails for more than 20 days.

"We're building great tent cities," Trump said Thursday. "We don't have to release them."[ix]

Detention Centers

Wil S. Hylton published on February 4, 2015, an extraordinary article in The New York Times Magazine, entitled: "Family Detention Camps: America's Shame[x]":

Christina Brown entered the refugee camp after an eight-hour journey through the desert. It was at the end of July last year; Brown was a 30-year-old immigration attorney. He had spent a few years after college working on political campaigns, but his law degree was barely a year old, and he had only two clients in his private practice in Denver. When other lawyers told him that the federal government was opening a mass detention center for immigrants in southeastern New Mexico, where hundreds of women and children would be housed in metal trailers surrounded by barbed wire, Brown decided to offer voluntary legal services to the detainees. I wasn't sure exactly what rights they might have, but I wanted to make sure they got them. She packed enough clothes for a week, stopped at Target to pick up coloring books and toys, and started driving south.

When he stopped in the dusty city of Artesia, he realized he still had no idea what to expect. The new detention center was just north of the city, behind a guard post in a sprawling complex with restricted access. Two other volunteers had been in town for about a week and had permission from federal officials to access the complex the next day.

Brown spent the night in a motel and then drove to the detention camp in the morning. He was in the windswept parking lot with the other lawyers, overlooking the barren plains of the eastern plateau. After a few minutes, a transport van emerged from the facility to pick them up. He pulled into the parking lot, and the lawyers moved on. They sat on the cold metal benches and peered through the caged windows as the bus drove back to the compound and through the bleak brown landscape. He pulled into a small trailer, and the lawyers left.

When they opened the trailer door, Brown felt a blast of cold air. The front room was empty, except for two small desks arranged near the center. A door in the back opened to reveal dozens of young women and children huddled together. Many were emaciated and malnourished, with dark circles under their eyes. "The kids were very sick," Brown told me later. "Many of the mothers held them, even the older children, held them like babies, and they screamed and cried, and some of them lay there indifferently."

Brown sat down at a desk and a guard brought a woman to meet him. Brown asked the woman in Spanish how she ended up being detained. The woman explained that she had to flee her home in El Salvador when the gangs were on their way to her family. "Her husband had just been murdered, and she and her children found his body," Brown recalls. "After he was killed, the gang started chasing her and threatened to kill her." Brown agreed to help the woman apply for political asylum in the United States, explaining that it might be possible to pay a small bond and then live with friends or family while she waited for an asylum hearing. When the woman returned to the back room, Brown was met by another, who was fleeing gangs in Guatemala. Then he met another young woman, who fled violence in Honduras. "They were all falling apart," Brown said. "They told us they were afraid to go home. They were crying, saying they were afraid of themselves and their children. It was a constant refrain: "I'll die if I come back." When Brown stepped out of the trailer that night, she already knew it would be hard to leave at the end of the week. The women he met were only a fraction of those inside the camp, and the government was making plans to open a second facility of nearly the same size in Karnes County, Texas, near San Antonio. "I remember thinking to myself that this was an impossible situation," she said. "I was overwhelmed and sad and angry. I think anger is what kept me going."

For the past six years, President Obama has sought to make children the centerpiece of his efforts to put a kinder face on U.S. immigration policy. Even though his administration has deported a record number of unauthorized immigrants, surpassing two million deportations last year, he has pushed for greater leniency toward undocumented children. After trying and failing to pass the Dream Act legislation, which would offer a path to permanent residency for immigrants who arrived before the age of 16, the president announced executive action in 2012 to block their deportation. Last November, Obama added another executive action to extend similar protections to some undocumented parents. "We will continue to focus law enforcement resources on the real threats to our security," he said in a speech on Nov. 20. "The criminals, not the families. Criminals, not children. Gang members, not a mother who is working hard to provide for her children." But the president's new policies apply only to immigrants who have been in the U.S. for more than five years; They do nothing to address the emerging crisis at the border today.

Since the 2008 economic collapse, the number of undocumented immigrants from Mexico has plummeted, while a wave of violence in Central America has brought a wave of migrants from Honduras, El Salvador and Guatemala. According to recent statistics from the Department of Homeland Security, the number of refugees fleeing Central America has doubled in the last year alone, with more than 61,000 "family units" crossing the U.S. border, as well as 51,000 unaccompanied children. For the first time, more people are coming to the United States from those countries than from Mexico, and they are coming not only for opportunity but for survival.

The explosion of violence in Central America is often described in the language of war, cartels, extortion, and gangs, but none of them capture the chaos that overwhelms the region. Four of the five highest homicide rates in the world are in Central American nations. The collapse of these countries is one of the greatest humanitarian disasters of our time. While criminal organizations such as the 18th Street Gang and Mara Salvatrucha exist as street gangs in the United States, in much of Honduras, Guatemala, and El Salvador they are so powerful and dominant that they have supplanted the government entirely. Opponents of these gangs, who routinely demand money for death threats and sometimes kidnap boys to serve as soldiers and girls as sex slaves, have no recourse to the law and no better option than to flee.

The U.S. immigration system defines a special pathway for refugees. To qualify, most applicants must appear before federal authorities, pass a "credible fear interview" to demonstrate a possible basis for asylum, and proceed through a "merits hearing" before an immigration judge. Traditionally, those who have completed the first two stages are allowed to live with family and friends in the United States while they await their final hearing, which may be months or years later. If authorities believe an applicant cannot appear for that court date, they may require the payment of a bond as collateral or place the refugee in a monitoring system that may include a tracking bracelet. In the most extreme cases, a judge may deny bail and keep the refugee in a detention center until the merits hearing.

There are close to 200 immigration detention centers in the United States, which are usually located far from major cities. Some house several thousand detainees at a time, mixing "Aliens" who have criminal records with others who don't.

The Justice Department released its first set of data on the incarceration rates of undocumented immigrants ordered by President Trump in an effort to build a case for more aggressive enforcement of immigration laws.

Of the 45,493 foreign-born inmates in the federal prison system made up of 188,658 inmates, the Justice Department said 3,939 are U.S. citizens.

According to the agency's data, immigration orders have been issued for 54.2 percent, approximately 22,541, of the remaining 41,554 immigrants incarcerated. Another 33.4 percent, approximately 13,886 inmates, are under investigation by U.S. Immigration and Customs Enforcement. For possible removal.

The Justice Department said about 12.3 percent, or 5,101, of illegal immigrants behind bars are still awaiting sentencing and 26 have received relief because they are at risk of persecution or serious harm if deported.[xi]

Immigration Courts in the United States

During a segment on April 1, 2018, Last Week Tonight host (John Oliver) exposed the pervasive injustice of immigration courts, particularly the ways in which they fail immigrant children.

Oliver showed a video of a child waiting for an immigration hearing, expressing fear that she and her family would be killed if she was sent back to her home country.

"That's horrible," Oliver said on the show, "because no child should have to worry about whether they're going to be killed. The biggest thing they should be concerned about is whether they can sit with the cool kids while eating their Tide Pods, and whether it can please Slender Man."

There are approximately 60 immigration courts in the country, governed by the Department of Justice. These courts rarely receive the same scrutiny or sustained media attention as ICE raids or other immigration-related legal processes. More troubling, "the system is a complete mess," Oliver said, citing current and former immigration court judges who acknowledged shocking flaws in "what sometimes goes through due process."

Case in point: Children as young as 3 or 4 years old are sometimes required to defend themselves in immigration court. "You can't teach immigration law to a 3-year-old!" Oliver exclaimed indignantly. "You can't even explain to a child that age that Elmo is not their best friend." Immigrants who may not speak English well also have to represent themselves instead of having access to an attorney.

Meanwhile, the rate of deportations often seems to vary wildly by region, with a deportation rate of nearly 90 percent in Atlanta. In other words, whether or not an immigrant is deported can arbitrarily depend on the city in which the trial is taking place. [xii]

You can watch the video by following this link:

Link a: Immigration Courts: Last Week Tonight with John Oliver (HBO)

4

EUROPE AND AFRICA

European Union

Asylum in the Member States of the European Union; it was formed more than half a century ago by the application of the Geneva Convention of 28 July 1951 relating to the Status of Refugees. Common policies appeared in the 1990s in relation to the Schengen Agreement (which abolished internal borders), so that asylum seekers who were unsuccessful in one Member State would not reapply in another. The common policy began with the Dublin Convention in 1990. It continued with the implementation of Eurodac and the Dublin Regulation in 2003, and the adoption in October 2009 of two proposals by the European Commission.

France

France was the first country to recognize the constitutional right to asylum, which is enshrined in Article 120 of the 1793 Constitution. The modern French right of asylum is recognized in the 1958 Constitution, in conjunction with paragraph 4 of the preamble to the 1946 Constitution, to which the Preamble to the 1958 Constitution directly refers. The 1946 Constitution incorporated parts of the 1793 Constitution that guaranteed the right of asylum to "any person persecuted for his action for liberty" who cannot seek protection in their countries of origin.

In addition to the constitutional right to asylum, the modern French right to asylum (droit d'asile) is enshrined on a legal and regulatory basis in the Code of Environment and the Law of Human Rights and the Law of Asylum (CESEDA). France also adheres to international agreements that provide for the modalities of application for the right to asylum, such as the 1951 United Nations (UN) Convention relating to the Status of Refugees (ratified in 1952), the 1967 Additional Protocol; Articles K1 and K2 of the 1992 Maastricht Treaty, as well as the 1985 Schengen Agreement, which defined the EU's immigration policy. Finally, the right to asylum is defined in Article 18 of the Charter of Fundamental Rights of the European Union.

Some of the criteria by which an asylum application may be rejected include: i) Passage through a "safe" third country, ii) Safe country of origin (an asylum seeker may be a previously rejected asylum seeker if he or she is a citizen of a country deemed "safe" by the French asylum authority

OFPRA), iii) Security threat (serious threat to public order), or (iv) Fraudulent application (abuse of the asylum procedure for other reasons).

The law of December 10, 2003 limited political asylum through two main restrictions:

The notion of "internal asylum": the application may be rejected if the alien can benefit from political asylum in a part of the territory of his or her country of origin.

The OFPRA (French Office for the Protection of Refugees and Stateless Persons) now lists so-called "safe countries" that respect political rights and the principles of freedom. If the asylum seeker comes from that country, the application is processed within 15 days and he or she does not receive welfare protection. They can challenge the decision, but this does not suspend any deportation orders. The first list, promulgated in July 2005, included Benin, Cape Verde, Ghana, Mali, Mauritius, India, Senegal, Mongolia, Georgia, Ukraine, Bosnia and Croatia as "safe countries". It had the effect of reducing the number of applicants from these countries by approximately 80 per cent in six months. The second list, adopted in July 2006, included Tanzania, Madagascar, Niger, Albania and Macedonia.

Although restricted, the right to political asylum has been retained in France amid several anti-immigration laws. Some people claim that, apart from the purely judicial route, the bureaucratic process is used to slow down and ultimately reject what could be considered valid applications. According to Le Figaro, France granted 7,000 people political refugee status in 2006, out of a total of 35,000 applications; in 2005, OFPRA in charge of examining the legitimacy of such applications granted fewer than 10,000 out of a total of 50,000 applications.

Numerous exiles from South American dictatorships, particularly from Augusto Pinochet's Chile and the Dirty War in Argentina, were received in the 1970s and 1980s. Since the invasion of Afghanistan in 2001, dozens of homeless Afghan asylum seekers have been sleeping in a park in Paris, near the Gare de l'Est train station. Although their demands have not yet been accepted, their presence has been tolerated. However, since the end of 2005, NGOs have noticed that the police separate Afghans from other migrants during raids and expel through letters those who have just arrived at Gare de l'Est by train and have not had time to demand asylum (a decree of 30 May 2005 obliges them to pay a translator to help them with official procedures).

United Kingdom

In the 19th century, the United Kingdom granted political asylum to a number of persecuted people, including many members of the socialist movement (including Karl Marx). With the attempted bombing of the Royal Observatory Greenwich in 1845 and the Siege of Sydney in 1911 in the context of propaganda of the actions of the (anarchist) facts, political asylum was restricted.[6]

Deaths in the Mediterranean

On July 3, 2018, Patrick Wintour, in his article published in The Guardian[xiii], reported that more than 200 migrants have drowned at sea in the Mediterranean in the past three days, bringing the death toll for the year to more than 1,000 and raising fears that human smugglers are taking greater risks due to the repression imposed by the Italian government and the Libyan coast guard.

The U.N. refugee agency in Tripoli reported Monday that 276 refugees and migrants were disembarked in the Libyan capital on Monday, including 16 survivors of a boat carrying 130 people, 114 of whom were still missing at sea. Other shipwrecks were found over the weekend.

On Tuesday, Libya's coast guard reported seven more deaths and another 123 migrants rescued.

The milestone of 1,000 deaths was reached on July 1. It is the fourth year in a row that more than 1,000 migrants have died trying to reach Europe via the Mediterranean Sea.

Othman Belbeisi, the chief of mission in Libya at the International Organization for Migration (IOM), said the "alarming increase" in deaths at sea was out of the ordinary. "Smugglers are exploiting migrants' desperation to leave before there are more crackdowns on Mediterranean crossings in Europe," he said.

Overall, the number of migrants arriving in Italy by sea has declined from last year's figures, but the proportion of those trying to reach Italy who are drowning is rising, raising claims that the Italian government's stricter policy is to blame.

Figures prepared by Matteo Villa, researchers at the Italian ISPI, show that so far in 2018, only half of those leaving Libya have arrived in Europe, compared to 86% last year.

The data shows that 44% have been recovered by the Libyan coast guard, compared to 12% last year. A total of 4.5% died or disappeared, compared to 2.3% last year. But in June, nearly one in 10 died or went missing leaving the Libyan coast, the highest proportion ever.

The Libyan Coast Guard has returned nearly 10,000 people to shore this year, according to IOM. That trend is likely to continue because of three policy changes by the new Italian government. It has closed the country's ports to NGO rescue ships; agreed to send 10 additional motorboat launches and two boats, boats, equipment and vehicles to assist the Libyan coastguard; and expanded the search and rescue area for which the Libyan coast guard is responsible, thereby reducing the area in which NGOs and EU vessels have responsibility.

The EU has also strengthened its guidance to NGOs to obey the orders of the Libyan coastguard. For the first time in months, no NGO ships are operating in the Mediterranean. The authorities detained two NGO vessels that docked in Malta and prevented them from leaving to carry out operations.

Italian Deputy Prime Minister Luigi Di Maio, a member of the Five Star Movement, said the deaths should not be used as evidence to dispute the government's tough new migration policy. "We will supply motorboats to Libya because the healthiest thing is that Libyans should carry out the rescues and bring the migrants back to the Libyan coast," he said.

The changes in Italian policy have increased the number of people in Libyan detention camps, which have been widely criticized by human rights groups and U.N. agencies.

Matteo Salvini, the Italian interior minister and the driving force behind the policy, has denied claims that Libyan detention camps are in overcrowded prisons, saying he has visited a detention center there and found conditions acceptable.

But IOM's Belbeisi said: "Migrants returned by the coastguard should not be automatically transferred to detention. We are deeply concerned that detention centres are once again overcrowded and that living conditions are deteriorating with the recent influx of migrants."

The UN says that up to 10,000 people are being held in detention camps.

At a briefing on Monday, a spokeswoman for the European commission said ships and vessels flying the European flag and carrying out rescues at sea could not take migrants to Libya.

"It is against our values, international law and European law," said Natasha Bertaud. "We are aware of the inhumane situation of many migrants in Libya. The UN is working to improve their conditions and there is an emergency transit mechanism in place to evacuate these people from Libya."

IOM Director General William Lacy Swing will return to Tripoli this week to see first-hand the conditions faced by migrants rescued and those returned to shore by the coastguard.

Overall numbers arriving in Italy are still down from last year, but Italy's populist government faces the problem of dealing with a backlog of more than 500,000 people whose asylum cases have not been processed.

So far, the leaders of Albania, Algeria, Egypt, Libya, Morocco and Tunisia have rejected the EU's main proposal to prevent migrants from reaching Europe (to establish asylum processing centres outside Europe). But the EU has yet to apply any serious pressure on these states, which rely heavily on EU aid.

5

OCEANIA AND ASIA

Myanmar Rohingya: What you need to know about the crisis[xiv]

Risking death by sea or on foot, nearly 700,000 have fled the destruction of their homes and persecution in Myanmar's northern Myanmar Rakhine province (Burma) for neighboring Bangladesh since August 2017.

The United Nations described the military offensive in Rakhine, which sparked the exodus, as a "textbook example of ethnic cleansing."

Myanmar's military says it is fighting Rohingya militants and denies targeting civilians.

Who are the Rohingya?

The Rohingya, who numbered around one million in Myanmar at the start of 2017, are one of many ethnic minorities in the country. Rohingya Muslims make up the largest percentage of Muslims in Myanmar, with the majority living in Rakhine State.

They have their own language and culture and say they are descendants of Arab traders and other groups who have been in the region for generations.

But the government of Myanmar, a predominantly Buddhist country, denies Rohingya citizenship and even excluded them from the 2014 census, refusing to recognize them as a people.

He sees them as illegal immigrants from Bangladesh.

Since the 1970s, the Rohingya have migrated through the region in significant numbers. Estimates of their numbers are often much higher than official figures.

In recent years, before the latest crisis, thousands of Rohingya made dangerous journeys from Myanmar to escape communal violence or alleged abuses by security forces.

Why are they fleeing?

The latest exodus began on August 25, 2017, after Rohingya Arsa militants launched deadly attacks on more than 30 police posts.

Rohingya arriving in an area known as Cox's Bazaar, a district in Bangladesh, say they fled after troops, backed by local Buddhist mobs, responded by burning their villages and attacking and killing civilians.

Rohingya crisis: refugees speak out about 'house-to-house' killings

According to Medecins Sans Frontières (MSF), at least 6,700 Rohingya, including at least 730 children under the age of five, were killed in the month after the violence erupted.

Amnesty International says the Myanmar military also raped and abused Rohingya women and girls.

The government, which puts the death toll at 400, claims that "clearance operations" against the militants ended on September 5, but BBC correspondents have seen evidence that they continued after that date.

According to Human Rights Watch's analysis of satellite imagery, at least 288 villages were partially or totally destroyed by a fire in Rakhine State, in the north of the country.

The images show many areas where Rohingya villages were reduced to smoking rubble, while nearby ethnic Rakhine villages were left untouched.

What is the magnitude of the crisis?

The UN says the Rohingya situation is the "fastest-growing refugee crisis in the world."

By August, there were already around 307,500 Rohingya refugees living in camps, makeshift settlements and host communities, according to UNHCR. An estimated 687,000 have arrived since August 2017.

Most Rohingya refugees arriving in Bangladesh (men, women and children with hardly any belongings) have sought refuge in these areas, setting up camp where possible in the difficult terrain and with little access to aid, clean water, food, shelter or medical care.

The largest refugee camp is Kutupalong, but limited space means that spontaneous settlements have sprung up in the camps surrounding and in the vicinity of Balukhali as refugees continue to arrive.

While numbers in Kutupalong refugee camp have dropped from a high of 22,241 to 13,900, the number of residents in makeshift or spontaneous settlements outside the camp has increased from more than 604,000.99,495 a

Most other refugee sites also continued to expand: as of mid-April 2018, there were 781,000 refugees living in nine camps and settlements.

There are also around 117,000 people staying outside camps in host communities.

6

VENEZUELA

Report on Human Rights in Venezuela 2017[xv]

Here's the executive summary of this report:

Venezuela is formally a multi-party constitutional republic, but for more than a decade, political power has been concentrated in a single party with a growing authoritarian executive that exercises significant control over the legislative, judicial, citizen, and electoral branches of government. The Supreme Court found that Nicolás Maduro won the 2013 presidential election amid allegations of pre- and post-election fraud, including government interference, the ruling party's use of state resources, and voter manipulation. The opposition won an absolute two-thirds majority of control of the National Assembly in the 2015 legislative elections. However, the executive branch used its control over the Supreme Court (TSJ) to weaken the constitutional role of the National Assembly to legislate, ignore the separation of powers, and allow the president to rule through a series of emergency decrees.

The civilian authorities maintained effective, albeit politicized, control over the security forces.

Democratic governance and human rights deteriorated dramatically during the year as a result of a campaign by the Maduro administration to consolidate its power.

On March 30, the TSJ annulled the constitutional functions of the National Assembly, threatened to abolish parliamentary immunity, and assumed significant control over social, economic, legal, civil, and military policies. The TSJ's actions triggered large-scale street protests during the spring and summer in which approximately 125 people were killed. Security forces and armed pro-government paramilitary groups known as "colectivos" sometimes used excessive force against protesters. Credible non-governmental organizations (NGOs) reported indiscriminate raids on homes, arbitrary arrests, and the use of torture to deter protesters. The government arrested thousands of people, tried hundreds of civilians in military courts, and sentenced about 12 opposition mayors to 15 months in prison for allegedly failing to control protests in their jurisdictions.

On May 1, President Maduro announced plans to rewrite the 1999 constitution, and on July 30, the government held fraudulent elections, boycotted by the opposition, to select representatives for a National Constituent Assembly (ANC). On August 4, the ANC adopted a "coexistence decree" that effectively neutralized other branches of government. Throughout the year, the government arbitrarily eliminated the civil rights of opposition leaders to not allow them to run for public office. On October 15, the government held gubernatorial elections that have been overdue since December 2016.

The ruling United Socialist Party (PSUV) maintained that it won 17 of the 23 governors' seats, although the election was plagued by shortcomings, including a lack of independent and credible international observers, last-minute changes to polling stations with limited public notice, manipulation of ballot designs, limited polling places in opposition neighborhoods and lack of technical audit for the tabulation of the National Electoral Council (CNE). The regime then called for mayoral elections on December 10, with numerous irregularities favoring government candidates.

The most important human rights issues included extrajudicial killings by security forces, including government-sponsored "colectivos"; torture by security forces; harsh and life-threatening prison conditions; widespread arbitrary detentions; and political prisoners. The government illegally interfered with privacy rights, used military courts to try civilians, and ignored court orders to release prisoners. The government routinely blocked signals, interfered with operations, or shut down television, radio, and other private media. The law criminalized criticism of the government, and the government threatened violence and detained journalists critical of the government, used violence to suppress peaceful demonstrations, and placed legal restrictions on the ability of NGOs to receive foreign funding. Other topics included interference with freedom of movement; the establishment of illegitimate institutions to replace democratically elected representatives; Widespread corruption and impunity among all security forces and in other national and state government offices, including at the highest levels; violence against women, including lethal violence; human trafficking; and the worst forms of child labor, which the government made minimal efforts to eliminate.

The government failed to take effective measures to combat the impunity that dominated all levels of the civilian bureaucracy and security forces.

Amnesty International Report 2017/18: Venezuela [xvi]

Venezuela remained in a state of emergency, repeatedly extended since January 2016. A National Constituent Assembly was elected without the participation of the opposition. The Attorney General was dismissed in irregular circumstances. Security forces continued to use excessive and undue force to disperse the protests. Hundreds of people were arbitrarily detained. There were many reports of torture and other ill-treatment, including sexual violence against protesters. The judicial system continued to be used to silence dissidents, including the use of military jurisdiction to prosecute civilians. Human rights defenders were harassed, intimidated and subjected to raids. The conditions of detention were extremely harsh. The food and health crises continued to worsen, particularly affecting children, people with chronic illnesses and pregnant women. The number of Venezuelans seeking asylum in other countries increased.

Background

The year was marked by growing public protests due to rising inflation and shortages of food and medical supplies. The state of emergency declared in January 2016 remained in place, giving the government special powers to deal with the economic situation. Despite the political dialogue processes initiated between the government and the opposition during the year, there was no concrete progress in advancing human rights issues.

Freedom of expression

The Office of the Special Rapporteur for Freedom of Expression of the Inter-American Commission on Human Rights (IACHR) expressed concern over the closure of 50 radio stations by the National Telecommunications Commission. Other media outlets also faced the threat of closure, despite a 2015 ruling by the Inter-American Court of Human Rights that declared such closures violated freedom of expression. Anti-government protesters and some opposition leaders were accused by the government of being a threat to national security. The government ordered the removal of some foreign news channels, including CNN, RCN and CARACOL from national cable TV operators. In September, unidentified journalists from the online news and investigations portal Armando.Info were threatened for their investigations into cases of administrative corruption.

Freedom of Assembly

Between April and July, in particular, there were mass protests for and against the government in various parts of the country. The right to peaceful assembly was not guaranteed. According to official data, at least 120 people were killed and more than 1,177 injured, including protesters, members of the security forces and bystanders, during these mass demonstrations. There were also reports from the Attorney General's Office that groups of armed individuals, with the support or acquiescence of the government, carried out violent actions against protesters. According to the local NGO Foro Penal Venezolano, 5,341 people were arrested in the context of the protests, of which 822 were tried. Of these, 726 civilians were subjected to military justice and charged with military crimes for demonstrating against the government. At the end of the year, 216 people remained in pre-trial detention.

Excessive use of force

In January, the government relaunched its public security program, formerly called Operation People's Liberation, under the new name Operation Humanist People's Liberation. Continued reports of excessive use of force by security officers. Amnesty International Report 394 2017/18 In the context of the demonstrations that took place between April and July, the government announced the activation of the "Zamora Plan", with the aim of "guaranteeing the functioning [of] the country [and] its security" by mobilising civilians together with police and military forces to "preserve internal order". However, details of the plan were not made public. The Bolivarian National Police and the Bolivarian National Guard, among other civil and military security forces, continued to use excessive and undue force against protesters. Between April and July, there was an increase in the deployment of military forces to suppress protests, resulting in an increase in the excessive use of less-lethal force and the misuse of lethal force, including the firing of tear gas directly at people's bodies, firing multiple rounds of ammunition, such as rubber bullets, beatings, and the use of firearms, all of which put protesters at risk of serious harm or death. According to the Attorney General's Office, Jairo Johan Ortiz Bustamante was killed by gunfire during a protest in the state of Miranda on April 6 and Juan Pablo Pernalete was killed by the impact of a tear gas canister in his chest during a protest in the capital, Caracas, on April 26. David Vallenilla, Neomar Lander and Rubén Darío González also died from injuries sustained during protests between April and July. During this period, the civil society organization Micondominio.com recorded at least 47 illegal raids on multiple communities and homes in 11 states across the country. These raids were characterized by the illegal use of force, threats, and arbitrary mass arrests, and were often linked to police and military operations against protests that took place near communities. The actions of the security forces during these raids were illegal and arbitrary and had indiscriminate effects. Armed groups also harassed and intimidated residents during the raids with the consent of the state security forces present. In August, the United Nations High Commissioner for Human Rights released a report highlighting the systematic and widespread use of excessive force during protests between April and July, pointing to a pattern of violent home raids and torture and other ill-treatment of detainees. The report also expressed concern about the difficulties faced by international organizations in accessing the country and the fears of victims to report abuses.

Arbitrary arrests and detentions.

Amnesty International documented 22 emblematic cases of people arbitrarily detained for political reasons through the implementation of various illegal mechanisms since 2014. These mechanisms included the use of military justice, warrantless arrests, and the use of ambiguous and discretionary criminal definitions, among others, which demonstrated a much broader pattern of efforts to silence dissent. By the end of the year, 12 of these persons received alternatives to detention; The other 10 remained arbitrarily detained, although the courts had ordered the release of many of them. These documented cases include those of MP Gilber Caro and activist Steyci Escalona, both members of the opposition party Voluntad Popular, who were arbitrarily detained in January after being publicly accused by top government authorities of carrying out "terrorist activities". Despite Gilber Caro's trial requiring the authorization of Parliament, he remained arbitrarily detained and his case was brought before military courts. Steyci Escalona was paroled in November. By the end of the year, none had been brought to trial. Hundreds of people reported that they were arbitrarily detained during protests that took place between April and July. Many were denied access to medical care or a lawyer of their choice and, in many cases, were subjected to military tribunals. There was a marked increase in the use of military justice to try civilians. In December, 44 people arbitrarily detained for what were considered to be politically motivated reasons by local NGOs were released with alternative restrictions on their freedom.

Torture and ill-treatment

Many new reports of torture and other ill-treatment were received. Wilmer Azuaje, a member of the Barinas state Legislative Council, was arrested in May. His family reported that during his detention he was locked in a noxious odor room, handcuffed for long periods of time, and sometimes held incommunicado, conditions that amount to cruel treatment. In July, the Supreme Court of Justice ordered his transfer to house arrest; however, at the end of the year, Wilmer Azuaje remained in the Detention Center on July 26 without charges against him or any improvement in his conditions of detention. During demonstrations between April and July, there were reports of ill-treatment by state officials during arrests of protesters, including kicking, beating, and sexual violence.

Human rights defenders

Human rights defenders and those seeking justice for human rights violations continued to be targeted and smeared in an apparent attempt to stop their human rights work. In February, lawyer Samantha Seijas was threatened by a police officer while filing a complaint at a police station in the state of Aragua accompanied by her daughter. In May, authorities raided the home of human rights defender Ehisler Vásquez in the city of Barquisimeto, Lara state. When he requested information about the reason for the raid, the Prosecutor's Office threatened to charge him with a crime. Later that month, in the same city, a group of unidentified individuals broke into the home of human rights defenders Yonaide Sánchez and Nelson Freitez. Human rights defenders were intimidated by state media and high-ranking government officials, who publicly announced their names and contact details while accusing them of "terrorism." Lawyers representing people on trial before military courts reported being harassed and intimidated by government authorities, putting a lot of pressure on those who defend people who criticize the government.

Justice System

The justice system continued to be subject to government interference, especially in cases involving people critical of the government or who were deemed to be acting against the interests of the authorities. The Bolivarian National Intelligence Service continued to ignore court decisions to transfer and release people in its custody. Two police officers from the municipality of Chacao have been arbitrarily detained since June 2016, despite an order for their release in August 2016. Another 12 officers charged in the same criminal case who had also been arbitrarily detained since June 2016 were released in December. In June 2017, the 14 officers began a hunger strike, some for 23 days, to demand that the authorities release them in compliance with the court order. In August, four opposition officials who had been elected to public office were arrested and five others received arrest warrants for them. These orders were issued by the Supreme Court in a procedure that was not enshrined in law. A total of 11 officials elected by popular vote were removed from office in irregular procedures.

Prisoners of Conscience

Leopoldo López, leader of the opposition party Voluntad Popular and a prisoner of conscience, was transferred to house arrest in August. During his detention at the National Center for Military Procedures in Ramo Verde, Caracas, there were several reports of abuses against him, including torture and denial of visits from his lawyers and family members. Villca Fernández, a student and political activist from the state of Mérida and a prisoner of conscience, was arbitrarily detained by the Bolivarian National Intelligence Service in Caracas. In her case, she was repeatedly denied emergency medical care and had reported other ill-treatment since her arrest in January 2016.

International Scrutiny

In May, Venezuela announced that it was withdrawing from the Organization of American States and therefore from the authority of the IACHR, further limiting the protection of victims of human rights violations in Venezuela. The decisions and rulings of international human rights monitoring mechanisms have yet to be implemented by the end of the year, especially in relation to the investigation and punishment of those responsible for human rights violations. In November, Venezuela received a visit from the UN Independent Expert on the promotion of a democratic and equitable international order. Visits by the UN Special Rapporteur on the right to development and the UN Special Rapporteur on the negative impact of unilateral coercive measures on the enjoyment of human rights were announced for 2018.

Enforced Disappearances

Former Defense Minister and detained government critic Raúl Isaías Baduel was unexpectedly taken from his cell at the National Center for Military Procedures in Ramo Verde, Caracas, on the morning of August 8; He remained missing for 23 days. The authorities acknowledged that he was being held at the facilities of the Bolivarian National Intelligence Service in Caracas, where he was held incommunicado and denied access to his family and lawyers for more than a month.

Impunity

Most victims of human rights violations continued without access to truth, justice and reparation. Victims and their families were often subjected to intimidation. In April, two officers of the Bolivarian National Guard were convicted of murdering Geraldine Moreno during demonstrations in the state of Carabobo in 2014. Most of the victims of killings, torture and other violations committed by state actors had yet to receive justice or reparation. The Attorney General's Office announced investigations into killings in the context of protests between April and July 2017. The National Constituent Assembly, established on July 30, appointed a Truth Commission to investigate cases of human rights violations during the protests; There were concerns about their independence and impartiality. There were reports of victims or their families being pressured by the authorities to testify and agree on facts that could absolve state agents of responsibility for these violations, as well as obstacles to the work of defense lawyers working with human rights organizations.

Detention

Despite reforms to the prison system in 2011, prison conditions remained extremely harsh. Lack of medical care, food and clean water, unsanitary conditions, overcrowding and violence in prisons and other detention centers continued. During clashes inside prisons, the use of firearms remained commonplace among inmates. Many detainees resorted to hunger strikes to protest against the conditions of their detention. The IACHR expressed concern over the deaths of 37 detainees at the Amazonas Judicial Detention Center in August during clashes that took place when the Bolivarian National Guard and the Bolivarian National Police attempted to search the premises.

Right to Food

The Workers' Documentation and Analysis Center reported that in December the basket of consumer goods for a family of five, which is used to define the consumer price index, was 60 times higher than the minimum wage, representing a 2123% increase from November 2016. Caritas Venezuela found that 27.6% of the children studied were at risk of malnutrition and 15.7% of them were severely malnourished. The government failed to acknowledge the worsening food shortages caused by the economic and social crisis. In its 2017 Global Report on Food Crises, the Food and Agriculture Organization of the United Nations stated that it lacked reliable official data on

Venezuela and that the deepening critical economic situation could lead to a greater absence of consumer goods, such as food and medical supplies.

Right to Health

After almost two years without publishing official data, in May, the Ministry of Health published the weekly epidemiological bulletins for 2016. The data revealed that during 2016, there were 11,466 deaths of children under one year of age, an increase of 30.1% compared to 2015, when this figure stood at 8,812. The most common causes of infant mortality were neonatal sepsis, pneumonia, and preterm birth. In addition, the bulletins showed that in 2016 324 cases of diphtheria were reported.

Women's Rights

The bulletins of the Ministry of Health indicated an increase in cases of maternal mortality of 65.8% between 2015 and 2016, with a total of 756 deaths registered in 2016, 300 more than in 2015. The lack of official data made it almost impossible to monitor the rate of femicides and other crimes against women. However, the NGO's Metropolitan Women's Institute estimated that there were at least 48 femicides between January and May. Ten years after the implementation of the Organic Law on Women's Right to Live Free from Violence, local NGOs reported that prosecutors, judges, police and other officials were still ill-equipped to protect women's rights, and women often suffered re-victimization due to institutional violence. Other obstacles to the implementation of the law include the lack of official data to plan and program public policies to prevent and eradicate violence against women.

Sexual and Reproductive Rights

The economic crisis continued to limit access to contraception. In June, in an online survey conducted by local NGO AVESA, 72% of respondents had not been able to access any contraceptives during the previous 12 months, and 27% said they could not buy contraceptives in pharmacies.

Refugees and Asylum Seekers

There was a notable increase in the number of Venezuelans seeking asylum in Brazil, Costa Rica, the United States, Spain, Peru and Trinidad and Tobago. Other countries in the region, including Colombia and Ecuador, also continued to receive large numbers of Venezuelans seeking refuge.

Human Rights Watch País Sumario: Venezuela[xvii]

Today in Venezuela, there are no independent government institutions that continue to act as a check on the executive branch. The Venezuelan government, under Maduro and previously under Chávez, has stacked the courts with judges who do not seek independence. The government has been cracking down on dissent through the often violent crackdown on street protests, jailing opponents and prosecuting civilians in military courts. It has also stripped power of the opposition-led legislature. Due to severe shortages of medicines, medical supplies, and food, many Venezuelans are unable to adequately feed their families or access the most basic medical care. In response to the humanitarian and human rights crisis, hundreds of thousands of Venezuelans are fleeing the country.

Other persistent concerns include poor prison conditions, impunity for human rights violations, and harassment by government officials of human rights defenders and independent media. Persecution of political opponents The Venezuelan government has imprisoned political opponents and disqualified them from running for office. At the time of writing, more than 340 political prisoners were languishing in Venezuelan jails or at the headquarters of the intelligence services, according to Foro Penal, a Venezuelan network of criminal law defense lawyers. In mid-2017, the Supreme Court sentenced five opposition mayors, following a summary process that violated international due process standards, to 15 months in prison and disqualified them from running for office. At the time of writing this article, one was at the headquarters of the intelligence services in Caracas; the rest had fled the country. At least nine 2 more mayors were subject to a Supreme Court injunction that could lead to similar prison sentences as the others if they are accused of violating them. Opposition leader Leopoldo López is serving a 13-year sentence for allegedly inciting violence during a demonstration in Caracas in February 2014, despite a lack of credible evidence against him. After three-and-a-half years in prison, López was transferred to house arrest in July 2017, but was arrested again in the middle of the night, weeks after he publicly criticized the government.

That same night, intelligence agents detained Antonio Ledezma, a former opposition mayor who has been under house arrest since 2015 and had posted a critical video while under house arrest. The Supreme Court later issued a statement saying López was barred from "political proselytizing" and that Ledezma could not "issue statements to any media," adding that "intelligence sources" said they had a plan to flee. Both men were returned to house arrest days later. In November, Ledezma fled Venezuela. Several others arrested in connection with the 2014 anti-government protests or subsequent political activism remain under house arrest or in pre-trial detention. The repression of protest activity by Venezuelan security forces, along with pro-government armed groups called "colectivos," have violently attacked anti-government protests, some of which were attended by tens of thousands of Venezuelans, between April and July 2017. Security force personnel have shot protesters with riot control ammunition, run over protesters with armored vehicles, brutally beat people who did not offer resistance, and staged violent raids on apartment buildings. The Attorney General's Office reported that as of July 31, 124 people had been killed during protest-related incidents. The United Nations High Commissioner for Human Rights reported in August that more than half of the deaths had been caused by security agents or colectivos. The Venezuelan government claims that 10 security force officers were killed in the context of the 3 demonstrations and reported several instances of violence against government supporters.

In late July, before the Constituent Assembly fired Attorney General Luisa Ortega Díaz, her office was investigating nearly 2,000 cases of people injured during the crackdown. While the number appears to have included cases in which protesters and security forces were the alleged perpetrators, in more than half of the cases, the office had evidence suggesting violations of fundamental rights. According to the Penal Forum, nearly 5,400 people were arrested in connection with demonstrations between April and November, including protesters, bystanders, and people who were taken from their homes without a warrant. About 3,900 had been paroled at the time of writing, but remained subject to criminal prosecution. Security forces have committed serious abuses against detainees, in some cases amounting to torture, including severe beatings, the use of electric shocks, asphyxiation, and sexual abuse. Military courts have prosecuted more than 750 civilians in violation of international law. By early 2014, the government had also responded to mass anti-government protests with excessive force. Security forces often held protesters incommunicado at military bases for 48 hours or more, and in some cases committed serious human rights violations, including severe beatings, electric shocks or burns, and forced detainees to crouch or kneel without moving for hours. No senior officer has been prosecuted for these abuses.

Constituent Assembly

In May, Maduro convened a Constituent Assembly through a presidential decree, despite the constitutional requirement to hold a public referendum beforehand to rewrite the constitution. The assembly is made up exclusively of government supporters elected through an election in July that Smartmatic, a British company hired by the government to verify the results, and later alleged was fraudulent. The Constituent Assembly has broad powers that go far beyond the drafting of a constitution. In August, as soon as the assembly began operating, its members assumed all legislative powers and fired Attorney General Ortega Díaz, a former government loyalist who had become an outspoken critic in late March, and appointed a government supporter to the position. In November, together with the Supreme Court, it stripped Freddy Guevara, vice president of the National Assembly, of his parliamentary immunity.

Operation People's Freedom

Beginning in July 2015, President Maduro deployed more than 80,000 members of the security forces across the country in an initiative called "Operation for the Liberation of the Peoples" (OLP) to address growing security issues. Police and military raids on low-income and immigrant communities led to widespread allegations of abuse, including extrajudicial killings, mass arbitrary detentions, mistreatment of detainees, forced evictions, destruction of homes, and arbitrary deportations. In November 2017, the attorney general said that more than 500 people were killed during PLO raids between 2015 and 2017. Government officials generally said the dead died during "clashes" with armed criminals, claims denied in many cases by victims' relatives or witnesses. . In several cases, victims were last seen alive in police custody.

Humanitarian Crisis

Venezuelans are facing severe shortages of medicines, medical supplies, and food, severely undermining their rights to health and food. In 2017, the Venezuelan health minister released official data for 2016 indicating that, in one year, maternal mortality increased by 65 percent, infant mortality increased by 30 percent, and malaria cases increased by 76 percent. Days later, the minister was fired. Cases of severe malnutrition among children under 5 years of age increased from 10.2 percent in February 2017 to 14.5 percent in September 2017, exceeding the World Health Organization's crisis threshold, according to Caritas Venezuela.

Judicial Independence

Since former President Chávez and his supporters in the National Assembly staged a political takeover of the Supreme Court in 2004, the judiciary has ceased to function as an independent branch of government. The members of the Supreme Court have openly rejected the principle of separation of powers and have publicly pledged their commitment to advancing the current administration's political agenda. Since the opposition assumed a majority in the National Assembly in January 2016, the Supreme Court has abolished almost all the laws it has passed. In March 2017, he assumed all legislative powers and partially backed down only after strong criticism in Venezuela and abroad.

Freedom of Expression

For more than a decade, the government has expanded and abused its power to regulate the media and has worked vigorously to reduce the number of dissident media outlets. Existing laws give the government the power to suspend or revoke concessions to private media if they are "convenient for the interests of the nation," allow for the arbitrary suspension of websites for the vaguely defined crime of "incitement," and criminalize the expression of "disrespect" by senior government officials. While some newspapers, websites, and radio stations criticize the government, fear of reprisals has made self-censorship a serious problem. Security forces detained, interrogated and confiscated the equipment of several journalists in 2017. Some international journalists were barred from entering the country or detained after covering anti-government protests or the health crisis. Several cable news channels and radios were taken off the air. In November, the Constituent Assembly adopted an "Anti-Hate Law" that includes vague language that undermines freedom of expression. It bans political parties that "promote fascism, hatred and intolerance", and imposes prison sentences of up to 20 years on those who publish "messages of intolerance and hatred" in the media or on social media.

Human Rights Defenders

Government moves to restrict international funding of nongovernmental organizations, combined with unsubstantiated allegations by government officials and supporters that human rights defenders seek to undermine Venezuelan democracy, create a hostile environment that limits the ability of civil society groups to promote human rights. In 2010, the Supreme Court ruled that individuals or organizations that receive foreign funds can be prosecuted for treason. That year, the National Assembly enacted legislation blocking organizations that "defend political rights" or "monitor the performance of public bodies" from receiving international assistance.

Political Discrimination

According to Venezuelan media reports, hundreds of government workers were fired in 2016 for supporting the ouster of President Maduro, and many others were threatened with dismissal in 2017 for supporting an unofficial plebiscite organized by the opposition against the Constituent Assembly proposal. Other reports say that a government program that distributes food and basic goods at limited prices by the government discriminates against government critics.

Prison Conditions

Corruption, weak security, deteriorating infrastructure, overcrowding, insufficient staffing, and poorly trained guards allow armed gangs to exert effective control over inmate populations within prisons. In August, 37 prisoners, nearly half of the detained population, were killed at the Amazonas Judicial Detention Center in Puerto Ayacucho and 14 security guards were injured when security forces tried to take control of the prison.

Key international players

In March and July, OAS Secretary General Luis Almagro presented two comprehensive reports on the humanitarian and human rights crisis in Venezuela, as part of ongoing discussions on compliance with Venezuela's Inter-American Democratic Charter, an agreement that protects human rights and democracy.

Between September and November, the OAS held a series of public hearings in which victims provided information to three experts who assessed whether abuses committed by

Venezuelan security forces could constitute crimes against humanity. In August, the regional trade bloc Mercosur suspended Venezuela indefinitely, applying the Ushuaia Protocol, an agreement that allows the bloc to suspend a member when there is a "rupture of [its] constitutional order." Also in August, 17 foreign ministers from the Americas met in Peru to address the crisis in Venezuela. Twelve of them, 11 Latin American governments and Canada, signed the Lima Declaration, a general declaration condemning the assault on the democratic order and the systematic violation of human rights in Venezuela. The 12 declared that they would not recognize either the Constituent Assembly or its resolutions, pledged to stop the transfer of arms to Venezuela, and expressed concern about the humanitarian crisis and the government's refusal to accept international humanitarian aid. They also indicated their willingness to support efforts towards credible and good-faith negotiations aimed at restoring democracy in the country in a peaceful manner. The Venezuelan government withdrew from the American Convention on Human Rights in 2013, leaving citizens and residents who can no longer request the intervention of the Inter-American Court of Human Rights when local remedies for abuses are ineffective or unavailable.

However, the Inter-American Commission on Human Rights (IACHR) continues to monitor Venezuela, applying the American Declaration of the Rights and Duties of Man, which is not an instrument subject to ratification by states. The United Nations High Commissioner for Human Rights released a report in August 2017, concluding that Venezuelan authorities had committed human rights violations and abuses in response to anti-government protests. The report says that "the widespread and systematic use of excessive force during demonstrations and the perceived arbitrary detention of protesters and political opponents indicates that these were not illegal or dishonest acts by isolated officials." In September, the high commissioner presented his findings to the UN Human Rights Council, saying that "crimes against humanity may have been committed" in Venezuela and calling for an international investigation. Numerous states expressed serious concern about human rights violations in the country. In 2015, U.S. President Barack Obama issued an executive order imposing targeted sanctions against seven Venezuelan government officials. In July 2016, the U.S. Congress extended until 2019 its authority to freeze assets and deny visas to officials accused of committing abuses against anti-government protesters during the 2014 protests. In 2017, the U.S. government issued additional sanctions against key Venezuelan officials, including President Maduro, as well as financial sanctions including a ban on transactions with new stocks and bonds issued by the Venezuelan government and its state-owned oil company.

President Trump threatened in August 2017 to use military force against Venezuela, however, he was the subject of widespread criticism in the region. The European Union has repeatedly expressed its concern about the deteriorating situation in Venezuela, condemning the violent repression of peaceful protests and the persecution of political opponents. In November, it imposed an arms embargo on Venezuela and imposed sanctions against Venezuelan officials. International efforts to mediate between the government and the opposition to restore democratic order in Venezuela have not yielded significant results. As a member of the UN Human Rights Council, Venezuela has regularly voted to avoid scrutiny of human rights violations in other countries, opposing resolutions highlighting abuses in countries such as Syria, Belarus, Burundi and Iran.

US sanctions[xviii]

The United States, in the face of the security threat that the so-called Bolivarian Revolution represents for the Region, has enacted the following legal measures against the dictatorship of Nicolás Maduro in that part of the Planet:

The Venezuela-related sanctions program represents the implementation of multiple legal authorities. Some of these authorities take the form of an executive order issued by the President. Other authorities are public laws (statutes) passed by Congress. These authorities are further codified by OFAC in its regulations, which are published in the Code of Federal Regulations (CFR).

Executive Orders:

- Executive Order: Blocking the Property of Additional Contributors to the Situation in Venezuela (November 1, 2018)
- 13835 - Prohibition of Certain Additional Transactions Regarding Venezuela (May 21, 2018)
- 13827 - Taking Additional Steps to Address the Situation in Venezuela (March 19, 2018)
- 13808 - Imposition of Additional Sanctions Regarding the Situation in Venezuela (August 24, 2017)
- 13692 - Blocking of Property and Suspension of Entry of Certain Persons Contributing to the Situation in Venezuela (March 8, 2015)

7

BUREAUCRACY

The Universal Declaration of Human Rights[xix]

The Universal Declaration of Human Rights (UDHR) is a landmark document in the history of human rights. Drafted by representatives with different legal and cultural backgrounds from all regions of the world, the Declaration was proclaimed by the United Nations General Assembly in Paris on 10 December 1948 (General Assembly resolution 217 A) as a common standard of achievement for all peoples and all nations. It establishes, for the first time, the universal protection of fundamental human rights and has been translated into more than 500 languages.

Preamble

Considering that recognition of the inherent dignity and of the equal and inalienable rights of all members of the human family is the foundation of freedom, justice and peace in the world,

While contempt and contempt for human rights have resulted in barbaric acts that have outraged the conscience of humanity, and the advent of a world in which human beings will enjoy freedom of speech and belief and freedom from fear and lack has been proclaimed as the highest aspiration. of ordinary people,

Considering that it is essential, if man is not to be compelled to resort as a last resort to rebellion against tyranny and oppression, human rights must be protected by the rule of law,

Whereas it is essential to promote the development of friendly relations among nations,

While the peoples of the United Nations in the Charter have reaffirmed their faith in fundamental human rights, the dignity and worth of the human person and the equal rights of men and women, and have resolved to promote social progress and better living standards in China. greater freedom,

Considering that Member States have undertaken to achieve, in cooperation with the United Nations, the promotion of universal respect for and observance of human rights and fundamental freedoms,

Considering that a common understanding of these rights and freedoms is of the utmost importance for the full realization of this commitment,

Now, therefore, THE GENERAL ASSEMBLY proclaims THIS UNIVERSAL DECLARATION OF HUMAN RIGHTS as a common standard of achievement for all peoples and all nations, to the end that every individual and every organ of society, having this Declaration constantly in mind, shall strive for teaching and education to promote respect for these rights and freedoms and by progressive measures, national and international countries, to ensure their universal and effective recognition and observance, both among the peoples of the Member States and among the peoples of the territories under their jurisdiction.

Article 1.

All human beings are born free and equal in dignity and rights. They are endowed with reason and conscience and must act with one another in a spirit of brotherhood.

Article 2.

Everyone is entitled to all the rights and freedoms set forth in this Declaration, without distinction of any kind, such as race, color, sex, language, religion, political or other opinion, national or social origin, property, birth, or other status. In addition, no distinction shall be made on the basis of the political, jurisdictional or international status of the country or territory to which a person belongs, whether independent, trusted, non-self-governing or under any other limitation of sovereignty.

Article 3.

Everyone has the right to life, liberty and security of person.

Article 4.

No one shall be subjected to slavery or servitude; Slavery and the slave trade are prohibited in all their forms.

Article 5.

No one shall be subjected to torture or to cruel, inhuman or degrading treatment or punishment.

Article 6.

Everyone has the right to recognition everywhere as a person before the law.

Article 7.

Everyone is equal before the law and is entitled without discrimination to equal protection of the law. Everyone is entitled to equal protection against any discrimination in violation of this Declaration and against any incitement to such discrimination.

Article 8.

Everyone has the right to an effective remedy by the competent national courts for acts that violate the fundamental rights granted to him or her by the Constitution or the law.

Article 9.

No one shall be subjected to arbitrary detention, detention or exile.

Article 10.

Everyone has the right, in full equality, to a fair and public hearing by an independent and impartial tribunal, in the determination of their rights and obligations and of any criminal charges against them.

Article 11.

(1) Every person charged with a criminal offence has the right to be presumed innocent until proven guilty in accordance with the law in a public trial in which he has been afforded all the guarantees necessary for his defence.

(2) No one shall be convicted of any criminal offence for an act or omission which does not constitute a criminal offence under national or international law at the time it was committed. Nor shall a more severe penalty be imposed than that which was applied at the time the offence was committed.

Article 12.

No one shall be subjected to arbitrary interference with his privacy, family, home or correspondence, or to attacks on his honour and reputation. Everyone has the right to the protection of the law against such interference or attacks.

Article 13.

(1) Everyone has the right to freedom of movement and residence within the boundaries of each state.

(2) Everyone has the right to leave any country, including his own, and to return to his country.

Article 14.

(1) Everyone has the right to seek and enjoy asylum from persecution in other countries.

(2) This right cannot be invoked in the case of prosecutions genuinely arising from non-political offences or acts contrary to the purposes and principles of the United Nations.

Article 15.

(1) Everyone has the right to a nationality.

(2) No one shall be arbitrarily deprived of his nationality or denied the right to change his nationality.

Article 16.

(1) Men and women of legal age, without any limitation on grounds of race, nationality or religion, have the right to marry and found a family. They have the right to equal rights in marriage, during marriage and at its dissolution.

(2) The marriage shall be celebrated only with the free and full consent of the future spouses.

(3) The family is the natural and fundamental group unit of society and is entitled to the protection of society and the State.

Article 17.

(1) All persons have the right to own property alone and in association with other persons.

(2) No one shall be arbitrarily deprived of his property.

Article 18.

Everyone has the right to freedom of thought, conscience and religion; This right includes freedom to change one's religion or belief, and freedom, either alone or in community with others and in public or private, to manifest one's religion or belief in teaching, practice, worship, and observance.

Article 19.

Everyone has the right to freedom of opinion and expression; This right includes the freedom to hold opinions without interference and to seek, receive and impart information and ideas through any media and regardless of frontiers.

Article 20.

(1) Everyone has the right to freedom of peaceful assembly and association.

(2) No one may be compelled to belong to an association.

Article 21.

(1) Everyone has the right to participate in the government of his country, directly or through freely chosen representatives.

(2) Everyone has the right of equal access to public service in his or her country.

(3) The will of the people will be the basis of the authority of the government; This will will be expressed in periodic and genuine elections to be held by universal and equal suffrage and to be held by secret ballot or by equivalent free voting procedures.

Article 22.

Everyone, as members of society, has the right to social security and has the right to the realization, through national effort and international cooperation and in accordance with the organization and resources of each State, of the economic, social and cultural rights indispensable for his dignity and the free development of his personality.

Article 23.

(1) Everyone has the right to work, to free choice of employment, to just and favourable conditions of work and protection against unemployment.

(2) Everyone, without any discrimination, is entitled to equal pay for equal work.

(3) Every person who works has the right to fair and favourable remuneration which guarantees for himself and his family an existence worthy of human dignity, and which is supplemented, if necessary, by other means of social protection.

(4) Everyone has the right to form and join trade unions in order to protect his or her interests.

Article 24.

Everyone has the right to rest and leisure, including reasonable limitation of working hours and periodic paid holidays.

Article 25.

(1) Everyone has the right to a standard of living adequate for the health and well-being of himself and his family, including food, clothing, shelter, and necessary medical care and social services, and the right to security in the event of unemployment, sickness, disability, widowhood, old age, or other lack of sustenance in circumstances beyond his control.

(2) Maternity and childhood have the right to special care and assistance. All children, whether born in or out of wedlock, shall enjoy the same social protection.

Article 26.

(1) Everyone has the right to education. Education must be free, at least in the elementary and fundamental stages. Elementary education shall be compulsory. Technical and vocational education shall be made generally available and higher education shall be equally accessible to all on the basis of merit.

(2) Education shall be directed to the full development of the human personality and to the strengthening of respect for human rights and fundamental freedoms. It shall promote understanding, tolerance and friendship among all nations, racial or religious groups, and shall promote the peacekeeping activities of the United Nations.

(3) Parents have the prior right to choose the type of education to be given to their children.

Article 27.

(1) All people have the right to participate freely in the cultural life of the community, enjoy the arts, and share in scientific advances and their benefits.

(2) Everyone has the right to the protection of the moral and material interests resulting from any scientific, literary or artistic production of which he is the author.

Article 28.

Everyone has the right to a social and international order in which the rights and freedoms set forth in this Declaration can be fully realized.

Article 29.

(1) Everyone has duties to the community in which only the free and complete development of his personality is possible.

(2) In the exercise of his rights and freedoms, everyone shall be subject to such limitations as may be determined by law

for the sole purpose of ensuring due recognition and respect for the rights and freedoms of others and of complying with the just requirements of morality. Public order and general welfare in a democratic society.

(3) These rights and freedoms may not, in any case, be exercised contrary to the purposes and principles of the United Nations.

Article 30.

Nothing in this Declaration may be construed as implying for any State, group or person any right to engage in any activity or perform any act aimed at the destruction of any of the rights and freedoms set forth herein.

United States

Every year, people come to the United States seeking protection because they have suffered persecution or fear persecution because of:

- Race
- Religion
- Nationality
- Membership in a particular social group
- Political opinion

If you are eligible for asylum, you may be allowed to remain in the United States. To apply for Asylum, file a Form I-

589, Application for Asylum and Withholding of Removal, within one year of your arrival in the United States. There is no fee to apply for asylum.

You can include your spouse and children who are in the United States on your application at the time you file your application or at any time until a final decision is made on your case. To include your child on your application, you must be under the age of 21 and unmarried.[xx]

Immigration and Nationality Act of 1965

The Immigration and Nationality Act of 1965 (H.R. 2580, Pub.L 89-236, 79 Stat.911, signed into law June 30, 1968), also known as the Hart-Celler Act, changed the way quotas were allocated by ending the National Origins Formula that had been in effect in the United States since the Emergency Quota Act of 1921. Rep. Emanuel Celler of New York proposed the bill, Sen. Philip Hart of Michigan co-sponsored it, and Sen. Ted Kennedy of Massachusetts helped advance it.

The Hart-Celler Act abolished the quota system based on national origins that had been U.S. immigration policy since the 1920s. The 1965 Act marked a shift from previous U.S. policy that had discriminated against Southern Europeans.

By removing racial and national barriers, the Act would significantly alter the demographic mix in the U.S.

The new law maintained per-country limits, but also created preference visa categories that focused on immigrants' abilities and family relationships with U.S. citizens or residents. The bill set numerical restrictions for visas at 170,000 per year, with one quota per country of origin. However, immediate relatives of U.S. citizens and "special immigrants" were unrestricted.[xxi]

INA: ACT 208 - ASYLUM[xxii]

Sec. 208. (a) Authority to apply for asylum.-

(1) In general. - Any alien who is physically present in the United States or who arrives in the United States (either at a designated port of arrival and including an alien who is brought to the United States after being intercepted in international or U.S. waters), regardless of such alien's status, You may apply for asylum under this section or, where applicable, section 235(b).

(2) Exceptions. -

(A) Safe third country. - Paragraph (1) shall not apply to an alien if the Attorney General determines that the alien may be removed, pursuant to a bilateral or multilateral agreement, to a country (other than the country of the alien's nationality or, in the case of an alien who has no nationality, the country of the alien's last habitual residence) in which the alien's life or liberty would not be threatened on the basis of race, religion, nationality, membership in a particular social group, or political opinion, and where the alien would have access to a full and fair procedure for determining an application for asylum or equivalent temporary protection, unless the Attorney General determines that it is in the public interest for the alien to be granted asylum in the United States.

(B) Time limit. - Subject to subparagraph (D), paragraph (1) shall not apply to an alien unless the alien demonstrates by clear and convincing evidence that the application has been filed within 1 year after the alien's date of arrival in the United States.

(C) Prior asylum applications. - Subject to subparagraph (D), paragraph (1) shall not apply to an alien if the alien has previously applied for asylum and has been denied such application.

(D) Changed Terms. - An alien's application for asylum may be considered, notwithstanding subparagraphs (B) and (C), if the alien demonstrates to the satisfaction of the Attorney General, either the existence of changed circumstances that materially affect the applicant's eligibility for asylum or extraordinary circumstances, relating to the delay in filing the application within the period specified in subparagraph (B). (E) 7/APPLICABILITY: Subparagraphs (A) and (B) shall not apply to an unaccompanied alien child (as defined in section 462(g) of the National Security Act of 2002 (6 U.S.C. 279(g))).

(3) Limitation on judicial review.3/4 No court shall have jurisdiction to review any determination of the Attorney General pursuant to paragraph (2).

(b) Conditions for granting asylum. -

(1) In general. - (A) ELIGIBILITY: The Secretary of Homeland Security or the Attorney General may grant asylum to an alien who has applied for asylum in accordance with the requirements and procedures set forth by the Secretary of Homeland Security or the Attorney General in this section if the Secretary of Homeland Security or the Attorney General determines that such alien is a refugee within the meaning of section 101(a)(42)(A).

(B) BURDEN OF PROOF

(i) GENERALLY: the burden of proof is on the applicant to establish that the applicant is a refugee, within the meaning of section 101(a)(42)(A). In order to establish that the applicant is a refugee within the meaning of that section, the applicant must establish that race, religion, nationality, membership in a particular social group, or political opinion was or will be at least a central reason for persecuting the applicant.

(ii) SUSTAINED BURDEN: The applicant's testimony may be sufficient to sustain the applicant's burden without corroboration, but only if the applicant satisfies the fact that the applicant's testimony is credible, persuasive, and relates to specific facts sufficient to demonstrate that the applicant is a refugee. In determining whether the applicant has met the applicant's burden, proof of fact may weigh credible testimony along with other evidence of record. When the fact-checker determines that the applicant must provide evidence that corroborates credible testimony, such evidence must be provided unless the applicant does not have the evidence and cannot reasonably obtain the evidence.

(iii) CREDIBILITY DETERMINATION: Considering the totality of the circumstances and all relevant factors, a fact-checker may base a credibility determination on the behavior, candor, or responsiveness of the applicant or witness, the inherent plausibility of the applicant's or witness's account, the consistency between the applicant's or witness's written and oral statements (provided that it is made and whether or not under oath, and taking into account the circumstances in which the statements were made), the internal consistency of each statement, the consistency of such statements with other evidence in the records (including Department of State reports on country conditions), and any inaccuracies or falsehoods in such statements, regardless of whether an inconsistency, inaccuracy, or falsehood lies at the heart of the applicant's claim, or any other relevant factor. There is no presumption of credibility, however, if an adverse credibility determination is not explicitly made, the applicant or witness will have a rebuttable presumption of credibility on appeal.

(2) Exceptions. -

(A) In general. - Paragraph (1) shall not apply to an alien if the Attorney General determines that -

(i) the alien ordered, incited, assisted, or in any way participated in the persecution of any person on account of race, religion, nationality, membership in a particular social group, or political opinion;

(ii) the alien, having been convicted of a final judgment of a particularly serious felony, constitutes a danger to the U.S. community;

(iii) there are serious grounds to believe that the alien has committed a nonpolitical felony outside the United States prior to the alien's arrival in the United States;

(iv) there are reasonable grounds to consider the alien to be a danger to the security of the United States;

(v) the alien is described in sub-clause (I), (II), (III), (IV) or (VI) of section 212(a)(3)(B)(i) or section 237(a)(4)(B) (relating to terrorist activity), unless, in the case of an alien described in sub-clause (IV) of section 212(a)(3)(B)(i), the Attorney General determines, in the Attorney General's discretion, that there are no reasonable grounds to consider the alien a danger to the security of the United States; or

(vi) the alien was firmly resettled in another country prior to arriving in the United States.

(B) Special rules.-

(i) Conviction for aggravated felony. - For the purposes of clause (ii) of subparagraph (A), an alien who has been convicted of an aggravated felony shall be deemed to have been convicted of a particularly serious felony.

(ii) Crimes. - The Attorney General may designate for statutory offenses that will be considered offenses described in clause (ii) or (iii) of subparagraph (A).

(C) Additional Limitations. - The Attorney General may, by regulation, establish additional limitations and conditions, pursuant to this section, under which an alien shall not be eligible for asylum under paragraph (1).

(D) There is no judicial review. - There shall be no judicial review of a determination by the Attorney General under subparagraph (A)(v).

(3) TREATMENT OF THE WIFE AND CHILDREN.

(A) GENERALLY: a spouse or child (as defined in section 101(b)(1)(A), (B), (C), (D), or (E)) of an alien who is granted asylum under this subsection, if not eligible for asylum under this section, may be granted the same status as the alien if accompanying, or after joining, to said foreigner.

(B) CONTINUING CLASSIFICATION OF CERTAIN ALIENS AS CHILDREN: an unmarried alien seeking to accompany or follow to join, a parent who was granted asylum under this subsection and who was under the age of 21 on the date such parent applied for asylum under this section, shall continue to be classified as a child for purposes of this paragraph and section 209(b)(3), if the alien turned 21 years of age after the application was filed but while it was pending.

(C) INITIAL JURISDICTION- An asylum officer (as defined in section 235(b)(1)(E)) shall have initial jurisdiction over any application for asylum filed by an unaccompanied alien child (as defined in section 462(g) of the Homeland Security Act of 2002 (6 U.S.C. 279(g)), regardless of whether filed pursuant to this section or section 235(b)).

(c) Asylum status. -

(1) In general.- In the case of an alien who is granted asylum under subsection (b), the Attorney General shall:

(A) shall not remove or return the alien to the alien's country of nationality or, in the case of a person who is not a national, the country of the alien's last habitual residence;

(B) authorize the alien to perform employment in the United States and provide the alien with appropriate support for that authorization; and

(C) may permit the alien to travel abroad with the prior consent of the Attorney General.

(2) Termination of Asylum. - Asylum granted under subsection (b) does not convey the right to remain permanently in the United States, and may be terminated if the Attorney General determines that -

(A) the alien no longer meets the conditions described in subsection (b)(1) due to a fundamental change in circumstances;

(B) the alien meets a condition described in subsection (b)(2);

(C) the alien may be transferred, pursuant to a bilateral or multilateral agreement, to a country (other than the country of the alien's nationality or, in the case of an alien without nationality, the country of the alien's last habitual residence) in which the alien's life or liberty would not be threatened on grounds of race, religion, nationality, membership in a particular social group or political opinion, and where the alien is eligible to receive asylum or equivalent temporary protection;

(D) the alien has voluntarily availed himself of the protection of the alien's country of nationality or, in the case of an alien who is not a national, the alien's country of habitual residence, upon returning to that country with permanent resident status or the reasonable possibility of obtaining such status with the same rights and obligations as other permanent residents of that country; or

(E) the alien has acquired a new nationality and enjoys the protection of the country of his or her new nationality.

(3) Removal when asylum is terminated. - An alien described in paragraph (2) is subject to any applicable ground of inadmissibility or deportability under section 212(a) and 237(a), and the removal or return of the alien shall be directed by the Attorney General pursuant to sections 240 and 241.

(d) Asylum procedure. -

(1) Applications. - The Attorney General shall establish a procedure for the consideration of asylum applications submitted under subsection (a). The Attorney General may require applicants to submit fingerprints and a photograph at that time and in such manner as the Attorney General may determine.

(2) Employment. - An asylum seeker is not entitled to employment authorization, but such authorization may be provided under the regulation of the Attorney General. An applicant who is not eligible for employment authorization

will not be granted such authorization before 180 days from the date of submission of the asylum application.

(3) Fees. - The Attorney General may impose fees for consideration of an asylum application, for employment authorization under this section, and for adjustment of status under section 209(b). Such fees shall not exceed the Attorney General's costs in adjudicating applications. The Attorney General may provide for the assessment and payment of such fees over a period of time or in installments. Nothing in this paragraph shall be construed to require the Attorney General to charge fees for adjudication services to asylum seekers, or to limit the Attorney General's authority to set adjudication and naturalization fees in accordance with section 286(m).

(4) Notice of Attorney Privilege and Consequences of Frivolous Enforcement. - When filing an application for asylum, the Attorney General must:

(A) notifies the alien of the privilege of being represented by counsel and the consequences, pursuant to paragraph (6), of knowingly making a frivolous application for asylum; and

(B) provide the alien with a list of persons (updated not less than once a quarter) who have indicated their availability to represent aliens in asylum proceedings free of charge.

(5) Consideration of asylum applications. -

(A) Procedures. - The procedure set forth in paragraph (1) shall provide that: (i) asylum may not be granted until the identity of the applicant has been verified against all appropriate records or databases maintained by the Attorney General and the Secretary of State, including the Visa Lookout System, to determine the grounds on which the alien may be inadmissible or deported from the United States, or not be eligible to apply for or receive asylum;

(ii) in the absence of exceptional circumstances, the initial interview or hearing on the asylum application shall commence no later than 45 days after the date of submission of the application;

(iii) in the absence of exceptional circumstances, the final administrative adjudication of the asylum application, not including the administrative appeal, shall be completed within 180 days of the date of submission of the application;

(iv) any administrative appeal must be filed within 30 days of the decision granting or denying asylum, or within 30 days after the completion of removal proceedings before a section 240 immigration judge, whichever is later; and

(v) In the case of an asylum applicant who fails to produce prior authorization or in the absence of exceptional circumstances to appear for an interview or hearing, including a hearing under section 240, the application may be rejected or the applicant may otherwise be penalized for such failure.

(B) Additional Regulatory Conditions. - The Attorney General may establish by regulation any other condition or limitation in the consideration of an application for asylum that is not incompatible with this Act.

(6) Frivolous applications. - If the Attorney General determines that an alien has knowingly filed a frivolous application for asylum and the alien has received notice pursuant to paragraph (4)(A), the alien shall not be eligible for any benefit under this Act, effective as of the date of a final determination on such application.

(7) There is no private right of action. - Nothing in this subsection shall be construed to create any substantive or procedural right or benefit that is legally enforceable by either party against the United States or its agencies or officers or any other person.

(e) Northern Mariana Islands Community-

The provisions of this section and section 209(b) shall apply to persons physically present in the Commonwealth of the Northern Mariana Islands or arriving in the Commonwealth (whether at a designated port of arrival and including persons who are brought into the Commonwealth after being intercepted in international or United States waters) only on or after January 1, 2014.

Europe

Admissibility, Liability and Security in Asylum Procedures in Europe[xxiii]

In compliance with their international obligations, European and EU states have developed sophisticated asylum systems based on complex procedural tools. In some cases, the tools are designed and used in order to avoid liability for refugees, as they allow claims to be deemed inadmissible before the content of the claim is analysed. The recent agreement between the EU and Turkey and the European Commission's proposal for harmonised asylum procedures under an Asylum Procedures Regulation, for example, revolve around concepts such as "safe third country" and "first country of asylum". A report launched today by the Asylum Information Database (AIDA), managed by the European Council on Refugees and Exiles (ECRE), documents the limited and fragmented application of the concepts of admissibility and safe country in 20 European countries.

"The latest reform of the European Common Asylum System puts the concepts of admissibility, responsibility and security at the forefront of European asylum procedures, by introducing the obligation for Member States to consider inadmissible applications on the basis of 'first country of asylum' and 'safe land of third countries,'" says Minos Mouzourakis, AIDA Coordinator. "However, such a move seems ill-suited in the absence of evidence-based knowledge about the use and interpretation of these concepts across the continent."

The recent introduction of comprehensive lists of "safe third countries" in countries such as Hungary, as well as the pressure on Greece to implement the concept following the EU-Turkey agreement, runs counter to the practice in countries with safe country concepts that are more entrenched in asylum procedures. Countries with more experience and often judicial guidance in applying the concept of a "safe third country" have clarified that an asylum seeker cannot be considered to have a "sufficient connection" to a third country simply on the basis of transit or short stay.

The report also analyses the implementation of the Dublin Regulation and the emergency relocation plan, two instruments that regulate the allocation of asylum responsibilities within the EU. As far as relocation is concerned, despite extremely slow implementation rates in Europe, countries such as France and Portugal have designed processes for the rapid processing of claims from people relocated to their territory and their assignment to the different regions where applicants will be accommodated.

Based on the AIDA report, ECRE calls on European countries and EU institutions to:

Proactively publish detailed statistics on key elements of their asylum procedures, such as inadmissibility decisions and the application of the Dublin Regulation, to promote evidence-based discussions on the functioning and challenges faced by their asylum systems.

Maintain the 1951 Refugee Convention as the standard of international protection and apply the concepts of "first country of asylum" and "safe third country" only to an asylum seeker who has already been recognised as a refugee or can be recognised as a refugee under the Convention, and can effectively benefit from such protection;

To interpret the criterion of "sufficient connection" rigorously for the purposes of the concept of a "safe third country", in order to refrain from declaring asylum applications inadmissible on the sole ground that an asylum-seeker has transited through a country considered safe.

Firmly suspend the use of the Dublin procedure with respect to countries demonstrating human rights risks, in line with national and European jurisprudence. The clear suspension of the Dublin procedures will ensure legal certainty for asylum seekers, but also a more efficient administration and allocation of the administrative and financial resources of the national authorities;

Step up their efforts to meet the commitments set out in the Relocation Decisions, building on the experience and good practices developed by Member States implementing relocation to date. States should also refrain from initiating Dublin proceedings with respect to countries benefiting from the relocation scheme, Italy and Greece, as the application of the Dublin Regulation is counterintuitive to ease the pressure on those countries' asylum systems.

South Africa

Refugee and Asylum Status[xxiv]

GENERAL PROCEDURE: ASYLUM APPLICATION

An Asylum Seeker

Is a person who has fled his or her home country and is seeking recognition and protection as a refugee in the Republic of South Africa, and whose application is still under consideration.

In the event of a negative decision on your application, you have to leave the country voluntarily or you will be deported.

A refugee

It is a person who has been granted asylum and protection status under the terms of Article 24 of the Refugee Law No. 130 of 1998.

According to the 1951 United Nations Convention, a refugee may be a "convention refugee" who has left his or her country of origin and has a well-founded fear of persecution on the basis of race, religion, nationality, political opinion, or membership in a particular social group. .

Under the same convention, a refugee can also be a person "in need of protection" whose removal to his or her home country would personally subject him or her to a risk of torture or a risk to his or her life or a risk of cruel and unusual treatment or punishment.

Role of the Government of the Republic of South Africa

The Government of the Republic of South Africa has an obligation to provide protection to refugees and other persons in need of protection under a number of United Nations Conventions, such as the 1951 Convention relating to the Status of Refugees.

However, Convention refugees and persons in need of protection based on risk to life, or cruel and unusual treatment must have personally faced the risk throughout the country in question

Eligibility procedure: asylum seeker

A person enters the Republic of South Africa through a port of entry (a land border post, airport, or port), claims to be an asylum seeker, and is therefore granted a section 23 Permit which is a "non-renewable asylum transit" of the Immigration Act.

The permit is valid only for a period of 14 days and authorizes the person to present themselves at the nearest Refugee Reception Office to apply for asylum under the terms of section 21 of the Refugee Law.

The asylum seeker must provide:

- A Section 23 Permit
- Any proof of identification from the country of origin.
- A travel document if you are in possession of one

The asylum seeker personally submits his or her application at a designated Refugee Reception Office where an admissibility hearing is held. The following are done:

- The applicant's fingerprints taken in the prescribed manner
- Interpreter if insured (if needed)
- First interview conducted by a Refugee Reception Officer (RRO) and a duly completed BI-1590 form

Asylum Seekers

- Data and image of the applicant captured in the refugee system.
- An Asylum Seeker's permit (a section 22 permit) is printed, signed, stamped, and issued to the Asylum Seeker

The section 22 permit, which is valid for a period of six months, legalizes the asylum seeker's stay in the Republic of South Africa pending a final decision on their application. The RRO can extend the permit for another six months while the status determination process is ongoing.

The holder of the section 22 permit has the right to work and study in South Africa and is protected from deportation to his or her home country.

Refugee status determination

Before the permit expires, the asylum seeker reports to the Refugee Reception Office to:

A second interview is conducted by a Refugee Status Determination Officer (RSDO)

The RSDO proceeds with a fair adjudication of the application, makes a decision on asylum claims, and provides reasons for decisions. RSDO must at the conclusion of the status determination hearing grant asylum; or reject manifestly unfounded, abusive, or fraudulent requests; or refer any question of law to the Standing Committee on Refugee Affairs (SCRA).

When asylum (written recognition of refugee status) is granted, a refugee is usually granted a section 24 permit, which allows that person to stay for a specified period of 2 years in South Africa, and is renewable upon expiry of its validity after the review process by an RSDO. In this case, the refugee must write a letter requesting the extension of their refugee status.

You are also allowed to work and study in South Africa as long as the permit is valid.

Refugee Qualification Documents

A refugee must apply for a refugee ID at any Refugee Reception Office within 15 days in the prescribed manner. After receiving an ID, a refugee can apply for an UNCTD (United Nations Convention Travel Document) at any Refugee Reception Office in the prescribed manner.

An ID is free

Appeal and Review Process

In the event of a refusal, an asylum seeker or refugee who believes he or she has a well-founded fear of persecution but whose claim has been rejected, may decide to appeal the RSDO's rejection decision to the Refugee Appeals Board (RAB) in the prescribed manner within 30 days of delivery of the decision.

The Board of Appeals conducts an appellate hearing during which the appellant who is entitled to a fair hearing has the rights to be heard and to present his or her case in full. The Refugee Appeals Board is responsible for considering and deciding appeals on decisions made by RSDOs.

The RAB may, after hearing an appeal, confirm or overturn or substitute the RSDO's decision.

With respect to manifestly unfounded claims, the Standing Committee on Refugee Affairs (SCRA) reviews or confirms or overturns decisions made by RSDO and refers cases to RSDO for determination within 14 days, as well as generally monitors RSDO decisions.

Certification

The applicant must have 5 full years of continuous residence in the Republic of South Africa as an officially recognized refugee, not as an asylum seeker

Write a request letter explaining the reasons for applying for certification

Go to the initial refugee reception office where the asylum application was first filed and fill out the form. The Refugee Reception Office will ensure that the applicant meets all requirements.

The application will be forwarded to the Standing Committee on Refugee Affairs, which is the body established to certify whether or not the applicant will remain a refugee indefinitely.

If successful, the applicant will receive a "Certification" or Section 27C that will allow them to apply at any Domestic Affairs office for an "Immigration Permit" or a "Permanent Residence"

Legal instruments

Refugees Act, 1998 (No. 130 of 19998)

United Nations Convention relating to the Status of Refugees of 1951.

1969 OAU Convention Governing the Specific Aspects of Refugee Problems in Africa and the 1967 Protocol relating to the Status of Refugees

1993 Basic Agreement between the Government of South Africa and UNHCR.

Immigration Law

Service Standard

Applications can take up to six months.

Cost

There are no fees for eligibility and status determination interviews, as well as the issuance or renewal of section 22, section 24, and refugee identification. The service to asylum seekers and refugees is free of charge.

All asylum seekers are encouraged to report anyone who asks for money.

Australia

Asylum seekers who arrive in Australia without a visa are subject to a range of punitive measures that can significantly harm their mental health and overall well-being. These measures have also greatly affected their ability to meaningfully participate in the refugee status determination process. Include:

- Wait up to four years for the government to grant you permission to apply for protection
- The inability to apply for permanent residency
- The elimination of free legal aid (with few exceptions)
- The imposition of an expedited (fast-track) determination process without adequate procedural safeguards
- The indefinite inability to reunite with immediate family members.

There are approximately 30,000 asylum seekers affected by these measures, labelled by the Australian government as the so-called "legacy case number". The negative political rhetoric and community stigmatisation resulting from this group of asylum seekers have also had a detrimental impact on them.

People seeking international protection have endured traumatic experiences before arriving in Australia and their resilience is eroded by the punitive measures they experience in Australia. Many asylum seekers suffer from clinically diagnosable mental disorders, such as anxiety, depressive disorders, and post-traumatic stress disorder (PTSD).

UNHCR's Regional Representation in Canberra is closely monitoring this situation and working to promote respect for the international human rights of asylum-seekers in Australia.[xxv]

I avoid saying it, but I graduated as an Army Officer from the – long ago – respectable Military Academy of Venezuela. I loved that career and I like serving people and nature, but today it is a shame that a large percentage of my Army colleagues are sufficiently responsible for one of the harshest Humanitarian Crises that Venezuela has experienced since Colonization. After this sad experience that, at the time of publishing this book, November 2018 has not come to an end, and knowing the behavior of other Armies of countries such as Myanmar, North Korea, China, I sincerely believe that this type of Armed Organizations should disappear and/or use their Capabilities to save humans from poverty instead of keeping dictators or themselves in Power over the Armed Forces. inert bodies of their fellow inhabitants of the Earth.

NOTE TO THE FIRST EDITION: The second part of this book was entitled: **REMAIN SILENT,** The only right we have. Los Aliens Legales, published in 2023 the English version and 2024 the Spanish version.

THE AUTHOR

Juan Ramon Rodulfo Moya, **Defined by Nature**: Inhabitant of Planet Earth, Human, Son of Eladio Rodulfo and Briceida Moya, Brother of Gabriela, Gustavo and Katiuska, Father of Gabriel and Sofia; **Defined by society**: Venezuelan Citizen (Limited Human Rights by default), Friend of many, enemy of few, Neighbor, Student/Teacher/Student, Worker/Supervisor/Manager/Leader/Worker, Husband of K/Ex-Husband of K/Husband of Y; **Defined by the U.S. Immigration Office**: Legal Alien; **Classroom studies**: Master's Degree in Human Resource Management, English, Mandarin Chinese; **Real-World Studies**: Human Behavior; **Home Studios**: SEO Webmaster, Graphic Design, Application and Website Development, Internet and Social Media Marketing, Video Production, YouTube Branding, Part 107 Commercial Drone Pilot, Import-Export, Affiliate Marketing, Cooking, Laundry, Home Cleaning; **Work experience**: Public-

theasylumseekers.com

Private-Entrepreneurial Sectors; **Other definitions:** Bitcoin Evangelist, Defender of Human Rights, Peace and Love.

Publications:

Books:

- Why Maslow: How to use his theory to stay in Power Forever (EN/SP)

- Asylum Seekers (EN/SP)

- Manual for Gorillas: 9 Rules to be the "Fer-pect" Dictator (EN/SP)

- Why you must Play the Lottery (EN/SP); Para Español Oprima #2: Speaking Spanish in Times of Xenophobia (EN/SP)

- Cause of Death: IGNORANCE | Human Behavior in Times of PANIC (EN/SP)

- Politics explained for Millennials, GENs XYZ and future generations (EN/SP)

- Las cenizas del Ejército Libertador (EN/SP)

- Remain Silent: The only right we have. The legal Aliens (EN/SP)

- Fortune Cookie Coaching 88 Motivational Tips Made Of Fortune Cookies, Vol I (EN)

theasylumseekers.com

Blogs:

Noticias de Nueva Esparta, Ubuntu Café, Coffee Secrets, Guaripete Pro, Rodulfox, Red Wasp Drone, Barista Pro, Gorila Travel, Fortune Cookie Coach, All Books, Vicky Toys.

Audiovisual Productions:

Podcasts:

Ubuntu Cafe | Vicky Erotic Tales | Fortune Cookie Coach | All Books, available at: juanrodulfo.com/podcasts

Music:

Albums: Margarita | Race to Extinction | Relaxed Panda | Amazonia | Cassiopeia | Caracas | Arcoiris Musical | Close Your Eyes, disponibles en: juanrodulfo.com/music

Photography & Video:

On sale at Adobe Stock, iStock, Shutterstock, and Veectezy, available at: juanrodulfo.com/gallery

Social Media Profiles:

Twitter / FB / Instagram / TikTok/ VK / Linkedin / Sina Weibo: **@rodulfox**

theasylumseekers.com

Google Author: https://g.co/kgs/grjtN5

Google Artist: https://g.co/kgs/H7Fiqg

Twitter: https://twitter.com/rodulfox

Facebook: https://facebook.com/rodulfox

LinkedIn: https://www.linkedin.com/in/rodulfox

Instagram: https://www.instagram.com/rodulfox/

VK: https://vk.com/rodulfox

TikTok: https://www.tiktok.com/@rodulfox

TradingView: https://www.tradingview.com/u/rodulfox/

Where can I find Juan Rodulfo's books:

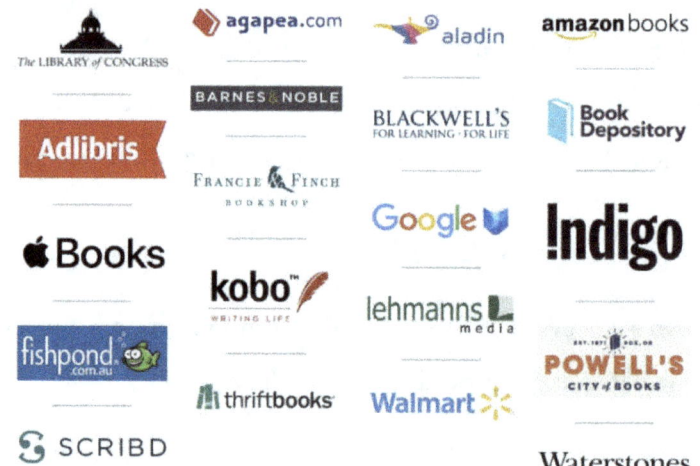

Barnes & Noble: http://bit.ly/3J8rbUP

Amazon Books: https://amzn.to/3yz0P9P

Apple Books: https://apple.co/3ZDLr84

Google Books: http://bit.ly/3yx3Ffy

Scribd: http://bit.ly/423ypCl

Agapea: http://bit.ly/3yuIuuj

Aladin: https://bit.ly/3LcYUiz

Adlibris: http://bit.ly/3J7oPmh

Blackwell's: http://bit.ly/3ZCZbQg

Book Depository: http://bit.ly/4247Gpa

Indigo: http://bit.ly/3TnJgDn

Fishpond: http://bit.ly/3J2cYZu

Kobo: http://bit.ly/3Tg4T8n

Lehmanns: http://bit.ly/3YJIvFs

Powell's: http://bit.ly/3ZIPb8m

Thriftbooks: http://bit.ly/3LgXXpM

Walmart: http://bit.ly/3Jc3rzm

Waterstones: http://bit.ly/3ZVevbn

Web Oficial: juanrodulfo.com

Endnotes

[i] Defined in the Cambridge Dictionary as "A country with a lot of industrial activity and where people generally have high incomes", Retrieved November 4, 2018 from:
https://dictionary.cambridge.org/us/dictionary/english/developed-country . The bdc website goes further with: "Developed countries have an advanced technological infrastructure and have various industrial and service sectors. Its citizens generally enjoy access to quality health care and higher education," Retrieved November 4, 2018, from: https://www.bdc.ca/en/articles-tools/entrepreneur-toolkit/templates-business-guides/glossary/pages/developed-country.aspx

[ii] Collins Dictionary, Retrieved November 04, 2018, available at: https://www.collinsdictionary.com/us/dictionary/english/political-asylum

[iii] Archaic English Legal Term meaning: Peace, security, or sanctuary imposed or guaranteed in early Medieval England

[iv] **Non-refoulement (/rəˈfuːlmɒ̃/)** is a fundamental principle of international law that prohibits a country receiving asylum-seekers from returning them to a country where they could be in danger of persecution because of "race, religion, nationality, membership of a particular social group or political opinion". Unlike political asylum, which applies to those who can prove a fear of persecution based on certain categories of people, non-refoulement refers to the generic repatriation of people, including refugees in war zones and other disaster places. It is a principle of customary international law, as it applies even to states that are not parties to the 1951 Convention relating to the Status of Refugees or its 1967 Protocol. It is also a principle of the trucial law of nations.

[v] The Law of Nations or the Vienna Convention on the Law of Treaties (VCLT) is a treaty that refers to international law on treaties between States. It was adopted on May 23, 1969 and opened for signature on May 23, 1969. The Convention entered into force on 27 January 1980. The VCLT was ratified by 116 states in January 2018. Some countries that have not ratified the Convention, such as the United States, recognize parts of it as a restatement of customary law and binding on them as such.

[vi] Sadof Alexander, 8 Dangerous myths about refugees debunked, (June 18, 2018), Retrieved November 04, 2018, from:

https://www.one.org/us/2018/06/18/dangerous-myths-refugees-debunked/?gclid=CjwKCAjwsfreBRB9EiwAikSUHeo2aGfhTuUUWyMvSiaBRfa9r6ypGOfyEhhSKJPIEIxhXNqcx78rQRoCY6cQAvD_BwE

[vii] Refugee Council, Top 20 facts about asylum, Retrieved November 4, 2018, from:
https://www.refugeecouncil.org.uk/latest/news/4548_top_20_facts_about_asylum

[viii] Wikipedia, Right of Asylum, Retrieved November 4, 2018, from:
https://en.wikipedia.org/wiki/Right_of_asylum

[ix] Nakamura David and Miroff Nick, The Washington Post, Trump announces plan to block some migrants from seeking asylum at the U.S. border Trump Announces plan to block some migrants from seeking asylum at the US-Mexico border, offers few details, (November 1, 2018), retrieved November 4, 2018 from: https://www/washingtonpost.com/political/trump-says-he-esl-finalizing-plan-to-end-abuse-of-us-asylum-system-chowing-mass-tent-cities-to-hold-migrants/2018/11/01/90fb6252-ddec-11e8-b732-3c72cbf131f2_story.html?utm_term=.2a122bfef78b

[x] Hylton Wil S., The New York Times Magazine, Los campos de detención familiar la vergüenza de los Estados Unidos [The Shame of America's Family Detention Camps], (February 8, 2015), Retrieved November 04, 2018 from:
https://www.nytimes.com/2015/02/08/magazine/the-shame-of-americas-family-detention-camps.html

[xi] Wheeler Lydia, DOJ Releases data on incarceration rates of illegal immigrants, (May 2, 2017), Retrieved November 4, 2018, from:
https://thehill.com/latino/331619-doj-releases-data-on-incarceration-rates-of-illegal-immigrants

[xii] Schonfeld Zach, John Oliver exposes the absurd injustice of Immigration Courts on "Last Week Tonight," (April 2, 2018), retrieved November 4, 2018, from:
https://www.newsweek.com/john-oliver-last-week-tonight-immigration-courts-868472

[xiii] Wintour Patrick, Mediterranean: more than 200 migrants drowned in three days, (July 3, 2018), Retrieved November 04, 2018 from:
https://www.theguardian.com/world/2018/jul/03/mediterranean-migrants-drown-three-days-libya-italy

[xiv] BBC News, Myanmar Rohingya: What you need to know about the crisis, (April 24, 2018), Retrieved November 04, 2018 from:
https://www.bbc.com/news/world-asia-41566561

[xv] Venezuela[xv] 2017 Human Rights Report, retrieved November 4, 2018, from:
https://www.justice.gov/eoir/page/file/1057096/download

[xvi] Amnesty International, Amnesty International Report 2017/18, retrieved 4 November 2018 from:
https://www.justice.gov/sites/default/files/pages/attachments/2018/03/06/ai_2018.pdf#page=393

[xvii] Human Rights Watch, Country Summary: Venezuela, (January 2018), Retrieved November 04, 2018 from:
https://www.justice.gov/eoir/page/file/1043001/download

[xviii] US Department of Treasury, Venezuela Related Sanctions, Retrieved November 04, 2018 from:
https://www.treasury.gov/resource-center/sanctions/Programs/pages/venezuela.aspx

[xix] UNITED NATIONS, The Universal Declaration of Human Rights, (December 10, 1948), Retrieved November 04, 2018 from:
http://www.un.org/en/universal-declaration-human-rights/

[xx] US Citizen and Immigration Services USCIS, Asylum, Taken November 04, 2018 from:
https://www.uscis.gov/humanitarian/refugees-asylum/asylum

[xxi] Wikipedia, Immigration and Nationality Act of 1965, Taken November 04, 2018 from:
https://en.wikipedia.org/wiki/Immigration_and_Nationality_Act_of_1965

[xxii] US Citizen and Immigration Services USCIS, INA: Act 208 Asylum, Taken November 04, 2018 from:
https://www.uscis.gov/ilink/docView/SLB/HTML/SLB/0-0-0-1/0-0-0-29/0-0-0-1687.html#0-0-0-192

[xxiii] Asylum Information Database (AIDA), Admissibility, responsibility and safety in European asylum procedures, (April 24, 2017), Retrieved November 04, 2018 from:
https://www.asylumineurope.org/2016-ii

[xxiv] Department Home Affairs Republic of South Africa, Refugee Status & Asylum, Taken November 04, 2018 from:
http://www.dha.gov.za/index.php/refugee-status-asylum

[xxv] The UN Refugee Agency (UNHCR), Asylum in Australia, Taken November 04, 2018 from: http://www.unhcr.org/asylum-in-australia.html

www.ingramcontent.com/pod-product-compliance
Lightning Source LLC
LaVergne TN
LVHW012252070526
838201LV00111B/339/J